TECHNOLOGY IN ANCIENT CULTURES

ANCIENT
AGRICULTURAL
TECHNOLOGY

FROM SICKLES TO PLOWS

Michael Woods and
Mary B. Woods

Twenty-First Century Books · Minneapolis

To the Rockefeller Foundation's Bellagio Center

Twenty-First Century Books
A division of Lerner Publishing Group, Inc.
241 First Avenue North
Minneapolis, MN 55401 U.S.A.

Website address: www.lernerbooks.com

Library of Congress Cataloging-in-Publication Data

Woods, Michael, 1946–
    Ancient agricultural technology : from sickles to plows / by Michael Woods and Mary
B. Woods.
        p.   cm. – (Technology in ancient cultures)
    Includes bibliographical references and index.
    ISBN 978-0-7613-6526-6 (lib. bdg. : alk. paper)
    1. Agriculture, Ancient—Juvenile literature. 2. Agriculture—History—Juvenile literature. 3. Food—History—Juvenile literature. 4. Food crops—History—Juvenile literature. 5. Agricultural innovations—History—Juvenile literature. I. Woods, Mary B. (Mary Boyle), 1946– II. Title. III. Series: Technology in ancient cultures.
    S421.W67 2011
    630.93–dc22   2010031146

Manufactured in the United States of America
1 – PC – 12/31/10

TABLE OF CONTENTS

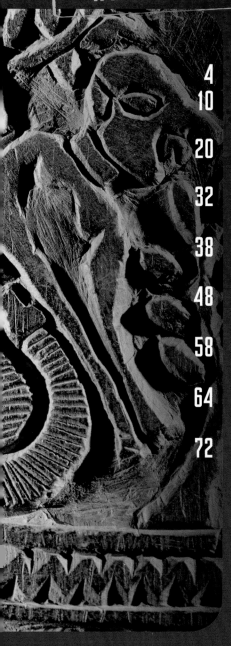

4   INTRODUCTION

10 CHAPTER ONE
    BEFORE AGRICULTURE

20 CHAPTER TWO
    THE ANCIENT MIDDLE EAST

32 CHAPTER THREE
    ANCIENT EGYPT

38 CHAPTER FOUR
    ANCIENT CHINA

48 CHAPTER FIVE
    THE ANCIENT AMERICAS

58 CHAPTER SIX
    ANCIENT GREECE

64 CHAPTER SEVEN
    ANCIENT ROME

72 EPILOGUE
    AFTER THE ANCIENTS

84 Timeline   91 Further Reading
86 Glossary   93 Websites
88 Source Notes   94 Index
90 Selected Bibliography

THE ANCIENT WORLDS OF AGRICULTURE

SCANDINAVIA

EUROPE

ASIA

ROMAN
EMPIRE

GAUL

ANCIENT
GREECE

Constantinople

ANCIENT
CHINA

Cosa

MESOPOTAMIA
(part of ancient
Middle East)

Rome

ITHACA

Thebes

Mediterranean Sea

Euphrates R.

PERSIA

Yangtze
R.

ANCIENT
INDIA

JAPAN

Tigris
R.

FERTILE CRESCENT

Babylon

ANCIENT
EGYPT

Nile
R.

AFRICA

INDIAN OCEAN

ATLANTIC
OCEAN

AUSTRALIA

INTRODUCTION

What do you think of when you hear the word *technology*? You probably think of something totally new. You might think of research laboratories filled with computers, powerful microscopes, and other scientific tools. But technology doesn't refer only to brand-new machines and discoveries. Technology is as old as human society.

NORTH AMERICA

GREAT PLAINS

N

ATLANTIC OCEAN

MESOAMERICA

CENTRAL AMERICA

SOUTH AMERICA

PACIFIC OCEAN

INCA EMPIRE

Andes Mountains

- ANCIENT INDIA
- ROMAN EMPIRE
- ANCIENT GREECE
- MESOAMERICA
- ANCIENT CHINA
- ANCIENT EGYPT
- INCA EMPIRE
- Ancient city
- Mountains

Technology is the use of knowledge, inventions, and discoveries to make life better. The word *technology* comes from two Greek words. One, *techne*, means "art" or "craft." The other, *logos*, means "word" or "speech." Ancient Greeks originally used the word *technology* to mean a discussion of arts and crafts. But in modern times, *technology* usually refers to an art, a tool, or a technique itself.

People use many kinds of technologies. Medicine is one kind of technology. Transportation and machinery are also kinds of technologies. These technologies and many others help make human life easier, safer, and more enjoyable. This book looks at a form of technology that has changed human life more than any other. That technology is agriculture, or farming.

Agriculture involves more than just growing crops. Agriculture is the practice of raising plants and animals to get food and other important materials. Growing fruits and vegetables, milking cows, sheering sheep's wool, and collecting honey from beehives are all examples of agriculture.

GAME CHANGER

Before people practiced agriculture, they were hunter-gatherers. They got their food by hunting game, fishing, and gathering wild plants. When the food in one area was all used up, the group moved to a new place.

After people began farming, they did not need to move from place to place to find food. They could settle in one spot. Some small farming settlements eventually turned into towns. Towns became cities. When people began living in cities, human society became more complex. Thus agriculture helped change the course of human history.

BEGINNINGS

Some of the first farmers on Earth lived in the Fertile Crescent. This was a crescent-shaped area of rich farmland in the ancient Middle East. The Fertile Crescent stretched through modern-day Israel, Lebanon, western Syria, southwestern Turkey, and central Iraq. People there began farming around 10,000 B.C. A few thousand years later, people in ancient China, ancient India, and the ancient Americas began farming. Gradually, farming technology spread around the world, although some groups continued hunting and gathering.

▲ This painting from an ancient Egyptian tomb shows a farmer cutting grain with a sickle. The tomb, near the ancient city of Thebes (modern-day Luxor), dates to the 1200s B.C. When people settled into farming villages, human society became more complex.

AGRICULTURE AND ARCHAEOLOGISTS

Ancient peoples left us many clues about their agricultural technology. Many ancient groups made pictures of farming, farm animals, and food processing. In many ancient cultures, people wrote about farming and the foods they ate.

Archaeologists are scientists who study the remains of past cultures. Archaeologists have found many clues about ancient agriculture. They have found tools that ancient people used to prepare food. They have found ancient knives for cutting meat, stones for grinding grain, vessels for carrying food, and ovens for baking bread. Sometimes archaeologists even find

▼ Ancient peoples made many of the same foods modern people prepare. This carving from an ancient tomb in Saqqara, Egypt, shows bakers making bread. The carving dates to around 2400 B.C.

remains of ancient food or drink itself. For instance, some ancient vessels have food smudges or stains inside. Archaeologists can test even the smallest smudge to figure out what substance the vessel once contained.

A LOT WITH A LITTLE

Ancient farmers did not have motorized equipment to help them work the soil and harvest crops. They did not use assembly lines to process and preserve food. But ancient peoples were true agricultural scientists. They experimented with new crops and growing methods. They bred, or mated,

▲ This Greek pottery vessel from 510 B.C. shows the harvest of grapes for wine making.

farm animals to produce offspring with special traits. They knew how to keep food from spoiling. They devised methods for making bread, cheese, wine, beer, olive oil, and other basic foods.

This book tells the story of this technology. Be prepared for some surprises. Ancient peoples ate some unusual foods, such as pigeon soup and boiled ostrich. But most ancient chefs prepared the same kinds of foods modern people enjoy. Read on and discover the history of many of your favorite foods.

CHAPTER ONE

BEFORE AGRICULTURE

Early hunter-gatherers fished in lakes, rivers, and oceans. They hunted and trapped animals. They gathered wild, edible plants such as nuts, acorns, grains, berries, and fruits. Sometimes they followed herds of wild animals from place to place.

Hunter-gatherers were also scavengers. They sometimes found food lying on the ground. Suppose a lion ate an antelope but left its bones and a little meat after the meal. Early humans probably competed with vultures and hyenas for these scraps. People used stones to crack animal bones to get at the rich marrow inside.

▼ Animal bones contain nutritious bone marrow. Ancient hunter-gatherers split these bones in half so they could eat the marrow inside.

Hunter-gatherers did not search for the tastiest foods. They were interested in quantity more than quality. Finding enough food was a matter of life or death for them. A steady supply of food was never a sure thing. During times of drought, or low rainfall, plants would not grow. Sometimes wildfires swept through large areas and killed both plants and animals. Often diseases struck certain animals or plants. When the food supply dwindled, ancient peoples starved and died. It's no wonder that ancient hunter-gatherers devoted much of their waking hours to the search for food.

NEW TECHNOLOGY

Over the centuries, humans developed new tools to assist them in hunting and gathering. They invented spears and bows and arrows for killing animals. They devised nets and traps for snaring fish and game. They learned to make razor-sharp stone knives to cut up meat. They used sharp sticks to dig up roots from underground.

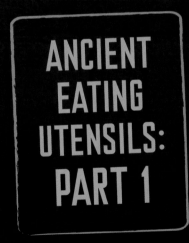

ANCIENT EATING UTENSILS: PART 1

Knives and spoons are almost as old as human society. Hunter-gatherers around the world used simple handmade knives to butcher meat. They probably used knives to cut food into bite-sized chunks as well. Hunter-gatherers might have used seashells or flat pieces of wood as spoons. They also ate with their fingers.

▲ A craftsperson in ancient France made this stone knife about ten thousand years ago. The knife might have been used to butcher meat.

At first hunter-gatherers ate only raw foods. About 400,000 B.C., hunter-gatherers in Europe began to use fire to cook food. Cooking makes food easier to chew and digest. It makes certain foods taste better. Cooking can also destroy poisons in some foods. For instance, a plant called manioc contains prussic acid, which can be deadly if eaten. But cooking manioc removes the poison. After ancient peoples in South America learned to cook manioc, the plant became a mainstay of their diet. Finally, cooking can kill harmful bacteria in food. Bacteria are tiny organisms that sometimes make people sick. Early peoples probably did not know about the health benefits of cooking. They just knew that cooked food was more appealing than raw food.

"He [an early human] has discovered the art of making fire, by which hard and stringy roots can be rendered digestible and poisonous roots or herbs innocuous [harmless]. This discovery of fire, probably the greatest ever made by man excepting language, dates from before the dawn of history."

—Charles Darwin, British naturalist, 1871

SOMETHING FISHY

Fish and shellfish were major sources of food for ancient hunter-gatherers. Around the world, archaeologists have found piles of ancient fish bones. Ancient hunter-gatherers no doubt ate the fish. But they had no use for the small bones. They piled the bones in heaps, like modern-day trash dumps.

Hunter-gatherers used wood, antlers, and animal bones to make fishing spears. The Cro-Magnon people, who lived in ancient Europe between thirty-five thousand and ten thousand years ago, made barbed fishing spears. Barbs are backward-facing points on a spearhead or an arrowhead. A fish can easily slip off an ordinary spearhead. But a barbed spearhead will catch in a fish's flesh, making escape difficult.

No one knows who invented the first fishhooks. It might have been the Cro-Magnons. People first made fishhooks from curved pieces of wood, bone, or shell. Later, people made hooks out of copper and other kinds of metal.

Ancient fishers probably tied hooks to vines or other ropes. They baited the hooks with insects. Peoples all over the ancient world—from Japan to Europe to the Americas—used this simple technology.

▼ This prehistoric carving of a salmon was found in a cave in France. Coastal peoples relied on fishing for much of their food.

The first fishhooks were J-shaped. They caught fish only when the hooks wedged securely in a fish's mouth or gills. Fish were often able to slip free of such hooks. Sometime around 5000 B.C., people in ancient Scandinavia (modern-day Denmark, Norway, and Sweden) invented barbed fishhooks. Like barbed spearheads, barbed fishhooks have points that project backward. The hooks stick firmly in place, even with a lot of tension on a fishing line.

Weirs are fencelike structures for catching fish in rivers. Early peoples made weirs out of vines, tree branches, or sticks pounded closely together. River currents swept fish into these traps. The fish couldn't escape, and ancient people were able to spear them or gather them in baskets. Ancient peoples also caught fish in nets made from vines and other plant fibers.

CONTAINERS

Hunter-gatherers needed containers to hold the fruits, nuts, and roots they collected. At first, people used natural objects as containers. People stored and carried food in dried gourds and big seashells. Even big, empty eggshells were useful containers. Ancient peoples also sewed up animal skins to make bags.

Ancient peoples used reeds, leaves, bark, and other plant fibers to weave baskets. Archaeologists don't know when the first baskets were made or who made them. But the technology probably dates to the earliest hunter-gatherers.

Hunter-gatherers in Japan made the world's first known clay vessel around 14,000 B.C. The round-bottomed pot was found at an ancient site in northern Honshu, the main island of Japan. Within a few thousand years, people in other ancient cultures had learned to make pottery. The process was simple. People shaped wet clay into bowls and other vessels. First, they dried the vessels in the sun. Later, people heated pottery in kilns, or big ovens. This process made the vessels stronger and more watertight.

FOOD PRESERVATION

Early peoples did not have electric refrigerators or freezers. But they devised many methods to keep food from spoiling. By studying ancient fish bones, archaeologists know that ancient hunter-gatherers sometimes treated fish with wood smoke. Chemicals in wood smoke can slow the growth of harmful bacteria in food.

In cold weather, early peoples probably packed food beneath snow and ice, which also slowed or stopped the growth of bacteria. Ancient peoples often dried food in the sun or over fires. This technique removed moisture that could serve as a breeding ground for bacteria in food.

GOING FOR THE GOLD

Archaeologists have learned a lot about ancient food and agriculture by studying cave paintings. In a cave near Valencia, Spain, an ancient hunter-gatherer drew a picture about twelve thousand years ago. The picture shows a man clinging to long vines or ropes. In one hand, he holds a basket. With the other, he reaches into a dark hole. The picture also shows a swarm of little dots emerging from the hole and flying around the man. Archaeologists believe the picture shows a man collecting honey. The dots are probably bees.

Ancient artists drew similar scenes in caves in many other parts of the world. The pictures show that honey was important to ancient peoples. People used honey as food. In some ancient cultures, people also used honey as medicine. They rubbed it on wounds to kill germs.

ANCIENT REFRIGERATORS

In ancient North America, early peoples hunted giant animals called mammoths. These animals, the relatives of modern elephants, contained thousands of pounds of meat. That was the good news for hungry hunter-gatherers. But a small band of hunter-gatherers could not eat all the meat from a mammoth at once. Sometimes ancient peoples simply left the extra meat for scavengers. But people also devised ways to keep the meat from spoiling.

Ancient hunters probably used snow and ice, smoking, and drying to preserve the meat of mammoths and other large animals. But a university professor named Daniel Fisher thinks they might have used another method as well. Fisher thinks that ancient hunter-gatherers used a technology called underwater caching (storage).

Underwater caching involves sinking chunks of meat into lakes and ponds. Under the water, cold temperatures, helpful bacteria, and low levels of oxygen keep the meat from rotting. In the 1980s, Fisher discovered butchered mammoth bones at the bottom of lakes in the midwestern United States. The bones suggested that ancient Americans used underwater caching to preserve mammoth meat eleven thousand years ago.

To prove his theory, Fisher and two coworkers performed an experiment. In the winter, they dropped pieces of lamb, deer, and horsemeat into the bottom of a pond. They also stored control, or comparison, samples in a modern freezer. The researchers periodically tested samples in a laboratory. After several months, they found the cached meat was just as well preserved as the meat stored in the freezer.

When hot weather arrived in June, the underwater caches of meat developed a strong odor and a sour taste. But tests showed that the meat was still nourishing. Fisher's re-creation of ancient technology showed that early residents of North America could have safely preserved mammoth meat for months.

ANIMALS STICK AROUND

One of the first steps on the road to agriculture was domesticating animals. Domesticating is similar to taming. Domesticated animals live among people instead of in the wild. By domesticating animals, ancient peoples got easier access to meat, eggs, milk, and fur. For instance, it is easier to raise pigs in enclosures and to slaughter them than it is to hunt wild pigs.

The first domesticated animals were dogs. Archaeologists think that people in the Middle East domesticated dogs more than twelve thousand years ago. At first, people probably kept wild dogs near their camps as watchdogs. Dogs scared away human and animal attackers, killed snakes, and kept mice and rats from eating stored food. People fed the dogs to keep them nearby. Wild dogs also accompanied hunters. With their excellent sense of smell, dogs were good at tracking game.

▼ Early peoples domesticated animals for many reasons. Donkeys, oxen, and horses could carry heavy loads and pull vehicles. Cows provided milk, meat, and leather. Chickens gave people eggs. Dogs were good hunters and guard animals. This stone carving, from around 2400 B.C., shows an ancient Egyptian with a hunting dog.

Gradually, people realized that they could breed dogs with the most desirable qualities. For instance, a hunter might mate a good male hunting dog with a good female hunting dog. Their offspring would also be good hunters. Generations of such breeding changed the very nature of dogs and other animals. Domesticated animals became physically different from their wild counterparts.

PEOPLE STAY PUT

Around the same time people began to domesticate animals, they also began to domesticate plants. Instead of gathering wild plants wherever they could be found, people learned to grow the plants they needed. They collected seeds from the crops they grew. They settled down and planted the same fields year after year.

▼ Ancient peoples got wool, meat, and milk from domesticated sheep. This painting shows a shepherd tending sheep in ancient Italy.

Agriculture transformed human society in countless ways. Once they were settled in one place, people began to build permanent homes. They marked off their farmlands with boundaries. Sometimes farmers grew more food than their families could eat. So farmers sold or traded the surplus. These transactions led people to create record-keeping systems, writing, and money. People also built roads and vehicles to help them carry goods from place to place. Eventually, small farm settlements grew to become big cities. As society became more complicated, people devoted more time to art, learning, and technology. They established laws and systems of government. In this way, farming led to the development of complex ancient societies.

Farming was hard work. Early farmers still had to worry about drought and disease, just as hunter-gatherers did. But overall, farming was a more reliable method of obtaining food than hunting and gathering. With better food supplies, people became healthier and lived longer. With the start of agriculture, Earth's human population nearly doubled. In 10,000 B.C., Earth had fewer than 3 million people. By 8000 B.C., the human population stood at 5.3 million. Historians refer to the many changes brought by farming as the agricultural revolution.

THE ANCIENT MIDDLE EAST

▲ This stone tablet from Mesopotamia shows ancient farmers.
Early farming settlements eventually became towns and big cities.

Earth has gone through many ice ages. These are long periods of cold temperatures, when much of the land is covered with sheets of ice. The most recent ice age ended around 11,000 B.C. When warm temperatures returned, enormous fields of wild wheat, barley, and other grains began to grow in the Fertile Crescent.

Hunter-gatherers in the Fertile Crescent began to rely on this wild grain for food. At first they probably just collected kernels (seeds) of wild grain. People cooked the grain or ground it up to make flour. Perhaps someone

▲ The first farmers on Earth lived in the ancient Middle East. This carving comes from ancient Sumer, part of Mesopotamia, and shows a man tending crops. The carving was made between about 3000 and 2685 B.C.

accidentally dropped some kernels in the mud and noticed that they later sprouted. They became new plants. People realized they could plant kernels intentionally to get the food they needed.

Slowly, the hunter-gatherer lifestyle began to change in the Fertile Crescent and other parts of the ancient Middle East. People settled down and grew grain. They raised animals as well as plants. After many years, farming people began to organize themselves. They created towns, laws, and economic systems.

One part of the Fertile Crescent was called Mesopotamia, which means "between rivers" in ancient Greek. Mesopotamia was between the Tigris and Euphrates rivers in modern-day Iraq. It was home to several ancient societies, including the Sumerians, Assyrians, and Babylonians.

This Sumerian panel from Ur, Mesopotamia, shows a banquet with a cow and a sheep. The panel is made of wood, lapis lazuli (a semiprecious stone), and shell and dates to 3000 to 2340 B.C.

GOATS AND SHEEP

Wild goats and sheep were abundant in the hills of the ancient Middle East. By domesticating these animals, early Middle Eastern farmers obtained milk, meat, and wool. Goats and sheep were fairly easy to domesticate. Both kinds of animals have strong herding instincts. They tend to stay in groups and follow lead animals. They rarely try to run away. Like most animals, baby sheep and goats form strong bonds with their mothers. But if a mother goat or sheep leaves or dies soon after a baby animal's birth, the baby will bond with and follow a human. By killing mother animals, ancient Middle Eastern farmers were able to get baby sheep and goats to bond with them.

Ancient Middle Eastern farmers learned to breed animals with desirable traits. If a farmer wanted big, even-tempered sheep that gave lots of milk, he mated animals with those characteristics. The farmer did not mate sheep that were small, aggressive, or poor milk producers. He butchered those animals for meat instead. Eventually, the farmer's herds consisted mainly of large, docile sheep that gave lots of milk.

THE PLOW

Plows are devices that cut into soil. Farmers use plows to cut long furrows, or trenches, in fields. Farmers then place seeds in the trenches. Archaeologists think ancient Middle Eastern farmers made the first plows soon after they began farming.

Farmers might have made the first plows from forked tree branches. A farmer used the forked end of the branch as a double handle. He sharpened the opposite end into a point. He used the handle to push or pull the sharp point through the soil. People soon realized that a plow works more efficiently if one person steers it while someone else pulls it with ropes.

Hooking up a plow to a large animal was even more efficient. Sheep and goats are too small and weak to pull plows through heavy soil. The strongest animals in the ancient Middle East were bulls, or male cattle. But bulls were too wild and violent to be harnessed to plows. Ancient farmers realized that they could tame wild bulls by castration, or removing their testicles. A castrated bull is called an ox.

Oxen were ideal for pulling plows. They could easily pull plows through hard-packed soil. They could plow more land in one day than a farmer could do on his own in one week. The first known picture of an ox comes from ancient Turkey. It is a wall painting made around 6500 B.C. It shows a bull without testicles. Archaeologists aren't sure whether people used this ox to pull a plow. The oldest pictures of oxen hitched to plows were made around 3000 B.C. in Egypt and Mesopotamia.

Ancient farmers learned to make sturdy plows out of wood and metal. Farmers improved plows by adding moldboards to the front. These curved metal plates not only dug furrows. They also lifted and turned the soil. In the process, moldboards dug up weeds, so farmers could easily remove them. Moldboards also churned up nutrient-rich soil from belowground, creating a fertile planting layer on top.

GARDEN PARTY

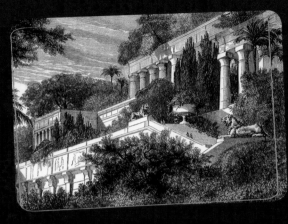

Agriculture was serious business in the ancient world. A successful harvest meant plentiful food for the coming year. A failed crop could mean starvation. But ancient people also grew plants just for pleasure. Gardens were common in ancient times. The Bible talks about the beautiful Garden of Eden, the home of Adam and Eve, the mythical first humans on Earth. Ancient writers also tell us about the magnificent Hanging Gardens of Babylon *(above)*. These gardens were built on top of terraces, or raised platforms. The plants and trees appeared to be floating above the ground. Throughout the ancient world, wealthy people planted other luxuriant gardens. Some rulers sent servants to neighboring countries to get especially rare, beautiful, or fragrant plants for their gardens.

MOVING WATER

Watering crops was hard work for ancient farmers. One gallon (3.8 liters) of water weighs about 8 pounds (3.6 kilograms). A typical ancient field needed thousands of gallons of water each day. Early Middle Eastern farmers used pottery jars and other containers to carry water from wells and rivers to their fields.

To make this job easier, people in Mesopotamia invented the shadoof. A shadoof is a long pole with a bucket on one end, a fulcrum (pivot point) in the center, and a weight on the other end. By raising and lowering the weight on a shadoof, a farmer could easily move a bucket of water at the other end of the pole. Farmers used shadoofs to hoist water from rivers. They poured

the water directly onto crops or into storage tanks. The first picture of an ancient shadoof comes from Mesopotamia. It was carved on clay and dates to around 2300 B.C.

ANCIENT KITCHENS

Excavations (archaeological digs) in modern-day Iraq show that Middle Eastern people used kitchens seventy-five hundred years ago. Archaeologists have found basic cooking equipment such as pots, jugs, and ladles in the remains of ancient farming villages. Ancient cooks also used flat stones for grinding grain into flour.

> "Again you will plant vineyards on the hills of Samaria [modern-day Israel and Jordan]; the farmers will plant them and enjoy their fruit."

—Hebrew Bible, first millennium (thousand years) B.C.

▲ Ancient Mesopotamians had fully equipped kitchens. This stone carving from ancient Assyria shows people preparing food and wine. The carving dates to about 865 B.C.

People in the ancient Middle East baked bread in big ovens. The ovens were made of clay that had been hardened by fire. Several families shared one oven. Bakers heated the oven with a wood fire. They placed flat loaves of bread against the oven walls for baking. Sometimes, bakers placed loaves on hot rocks in the bottom of the oven. Additional hot rocks placed on top of the loaves speeded up the baking process.

THE FIRST COOKBOOK

Archaeologists have found a series of recipes from ancient Babylon, which was part of Mesopotamia. The recipes were carved into two clay tablets. They date to around 1700 B.C. One dish featured small birds. Parts of the recipe are missing, so we don't know exactly what birds were used, but they might have been partridges. The recipe begins:

> Remove the head and feet. Open the body and clean the birds, reserving the gizzards [part of the digestive system] and the pluck

[organs]. Split the gizzards and clean them. Next rinse the birds and flatten them. Prepare a pot and put birds, gizzards and pluck into it before placing it on the fire.

The recipe also calls for leeks, garlic, onions, grain, milk, and oil. The end result was a kind of stew. The Babylonian recipes didn't give measurements or cooking times. They were probably meant for experienced chefs, who used their own judgment in cooking.

POTTERY

The agricultural revolution created a great need for pottery. Farming peoples needed vessels to hold water, milk, wine, olive oil, and other foods. People in the ancient Middle East learned to make pottery shortly after they began farming. At first Middle Eastern potters shaped pots by hand. They often used the coiling method, which involved winding long strands of clay to make the walls of a pot. Sometimes they simply pinched out the center of lumps of clay to make simple bowls.

In about 3500 B.C., people in Mesopotamia made an important advance in pottery production. They invented the potter's wheel. The wheel was a rotating wooden disk. The potter placed a lump of wet clay in the center. He or she turned the wheel while coiling or pinching the walls of the pot.

▶ This pottery vessel has a spout, so it was probably used for carrying and pouring liquid. It comes from ancient Iraq and dates to about 2500 B.C.

ANCIENT SPIRITS

Alcoholic drinks were common in the ancient world. Archaeologists have found beer residue inside a clay jar from Mesopotamia. The jar dates from between 3500 and 3100 B.C. The ancient Mesopotamian symbol for beer was a set of horizontal, vertical, or crisscross lines. The beer jar was marked with that symbol. The ancient Mesopotamians even worshipped a beer goddess named Ninkasi.

Wine was also popular in the ancient Middle East. In 1994 researchers at the University of Pennsylvania Museum of Archaeology and Anthropology in Philadelphia examined a yellowish residue inside two ancient jars from northern Iran. Tests showed that the jars were made between about 5400 and 5000 B.C. They are the world's oldest known wine jars.

But even these aren't the oldest known liquor bottles. In 2004 researchers at the same museum in Philadelphia examined ancient pottery jars from China. Tests revealed that the jars had held an alcoholic drink made from rice, grapes or another fruit, and honey. The jars date to 7000 to 6600 B.C.

To make alcoholic beverages, ancient peoples had to understand fermentation. During this process, bacteria, mold, yeast, and other organisms make chemical changes to food. Fermentation can change grape juice into wine, for instance. It can change mashed grain into beer, and milk into cheese and yogurt. Ancient beer and winemakers had to master the art of fermentation. They learned which substances caused foods to ferment and how long the process took. They became experts at making different kinds of beverages with different flavors.

The turning wheel allowed the potter to build the walls more evenly and faster than could be done by hand alone.

Ancient Mesopotamian potters hardened clay vessels by firing them in kilns. They also learned to coat pots with certain minerals before firing them. When heated, the minerals formed a glaze, or waterproof coating.

THE FIRST FABRICS

Making plant and animal fibers into fabric is a big part of agricultural technology. Fibers made from plants include cotton, flax, and hemp. The most widely used animal fiber is sheep's wool. People in the ancient Middle East used all these fibers to make fabric. They also used camel hair.

Turning fibers into fabric involves several kinds of technology. The first is spinning. Most natural fibers are very short. Cotton fibers, for instance, are only about 0.5 inches (1.25 centimeters) long. Spinning changes short pieces of fiber into long strands of thread or yarn.

Mesopotamians used tools called spindles and distaffs to turn fiber into

▼ Agriculture includes more than growing and preparing food. Making fabric is also part of agricultural technology. This clay tablet from ancient Iran shows a person using a loom to weave cloth. The tablet dates from 3300 to 3000 B.C.

yarn. A distaff is a small stick with a slot on one end. The slot holds clumps of fiber. A spindle is a long straight stick held between the thumb and the index finger. By twirling the spindle, a person carefully draws fibers off the distaff. The short fibers cling and twist together. They become a long strand of yarn.

The next step in making fabric is weaving. This craft involves interlacing two strands of thread or yarn at right angles. You can see this pattern yourself by looking through a magnifying glass at the tiny threads in cotton cloth. Weavers use a tool called a loom to hold the two sets of strands. Ancient Middle Eastern weavers used simple hand-operated looms. These small wooden frames kept one set of threads under tension while the weaver interlaced the crosswise threads.

Felt can be made without spinning or weaving. Felt is made from compressed wool fibers, locked together into a dense tangle. Felt forms naturally in the coats of sheep that are molting, or shedding. People can also turn loose wool into felt by wetting or heating the wool and pressing the fibers together. Felt was an important fabric in the ancient Middle East. People used it to make clothing, especially heavy garments for cold weather. The ancient Persians, based in modern-day Iran, made felt caps with earflaps.

TECHNOLOGY BREEDS TECHNOLOGY

Ancient Middle Easterners made dyes from plants, minerals, and animal secretions. They used the dyes to color clothing and other textiles. The ancient Phoenicians, who lived in modern-day Lebanon, made a beautiful purple dye. They called it Tyrian purple, after the Phoenician seaport of Tyre. The dye came from the glands of a shellfish. Rare and costly, Tyrian purple became a symbol of royalty and wealth in the ancient world. Kings and emperors wore clothing made from wool that had been dyed purple. In the Byzantine Empire, based in modern-day Turkey, the child of an emperor was said to be *porphyrogenitus*, which means "born to the purple" in ancient Greek.

Tyrian purple and other dyes presented a challenge for ancient Middle Eastern cloth makers. The wool of the first domesticated sheep was grayish brown. Such dark fabric wasn't good for dyeing. Dye doesn't show up on dark wool. To make Tyrian purple (or another color) fabric, a clothing maker needed to dye white wool. So shepherds needed to raise sheep with white coats. They solved this problem by mating male and female sheep with light coats. Their offspring also had light coats. By 1000 B.C., continuous breeding of light-colored sheep had led to sheep with white wool, which took the purple dye well. This same breeding technology also led to sheep with pure black or gray wool that required no dyeing.

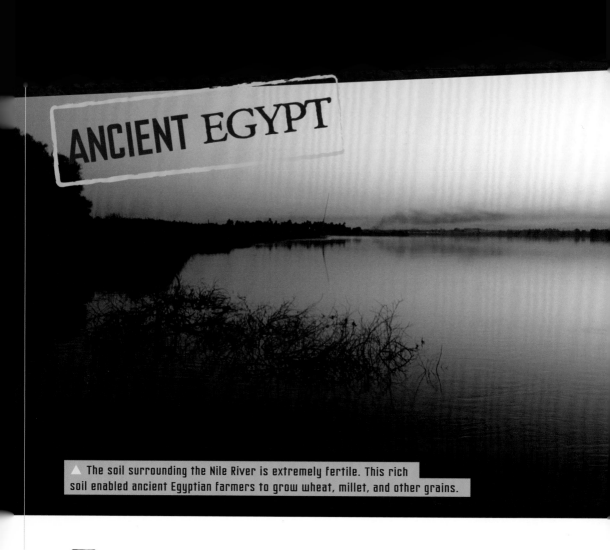

ANCIENT EGYPT

▲ The soil surrounding the Nile River is extremely fertile. This rich soil enabled ancient Egyptian farmers to grow wheat, millet, and other grains.

The Nile is the world's longest river. It flows from central Africa north to Egypt and the Mediterranean Sea. More than seven thousand years ago, ancient hunter-gatherers began to settle around the Nile in Egypt. People built permanent farms along the river. They grew wheat and other crops. Before long, a complex society had developed in ancient Egypt.

Every year, heavy rains fell in central Africa. The rains flooded the Nile. In summer the swollen river water reached Egypt and the Nile flooded its banks. The floodwaters soaked the dry soil. When the waters receded in autumn,

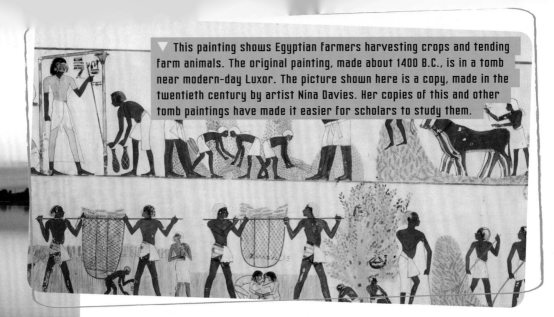

This painting shows Egyptian farmers harvesting crops and tending farm animals. The original painting, made about 1400 B.C., is in a tomb near modern-day Luxor. The picture shown here is a copy, made in the twentieth century by artist Nina Davies. Her copies of this and other tomb paintings have made it easier for scholars to study them.

they left behind muddy silt, or sediment. The silt was perfect for growing crops.

The ancient Egyptians learned about oxen, plows, and other farming technology from people in the Middle East. With this technology, Egypt became one of the greatest wheat producers in the ancient world. Egyptian farmers also grew cotton, millet (a kind of grain), and flax, which was woven into linen. Egyptian shepherds raised goats and sheep. Farmers also raised pigs.

BIG PROJECTS

Around 3100 B.C., a ruler named Menes united the people of Egypt under one government. He established Egypt's first dynasty, or ruling family. After unifying Egypt, King Menes began to build irrigation systems. Irrigation involves damming rivers, digging canals, building ponds, and devising other systems for moving, lifting, storing, and controlling water. Irrigated farmland yields about twice as much food per acre as nonirrigated farmland.

Around 2500 B.C., Egyptian engineers built a dam across the Nile River. It was the world's first human-made dam. Water backed up behind the dam, creating a large lake. The lake supplied drinking water to workers at a stone quarry south of Cairo. The dam was almost 350 feet (107 meters) long, 40 feet (12 m) high, and 78 feet (24 m) thick at the base. In another irrigation project, in about 2300 B.C., the Egyptians dug a 12-mile (19 kilometers) canal from the Nile to Lake Moeris. When the Nile flooded, water flowed through the canal to the lake. The lake served as a storage tank for the excess river water. Farmers used the water for year-round irrigation.

THE FIRST BEEKEEPERS

Ancient Egyptians used lots of honey. They put honey in food, applied honey to wounds, and offered honey as a gift to their gods. Ramses III, who ruled Egypt from 1198 to 1166 B.C., set aside 15 tons (14 metric tons) of honey for the gods in one year. The Egyptians needed much more honey than they could get by robbing wild beehives.

"They [Egyptian farmers] obtain the fruits of the field with less trouble than any other people in the world . . . since they have no need to break up the ground with the plough, nor to use the hoe, nor to do any of the work which the rest of mankind find necessary if they are to get a crop; but the husbandman [farmer] waits till the river has of its own accord spread itself over the fields and withdrawn again to its bed, and then sows his plot of ground . . . after which he has only to await the harvest."

—Herodotus, ancient Greek historian, 400s B.C.

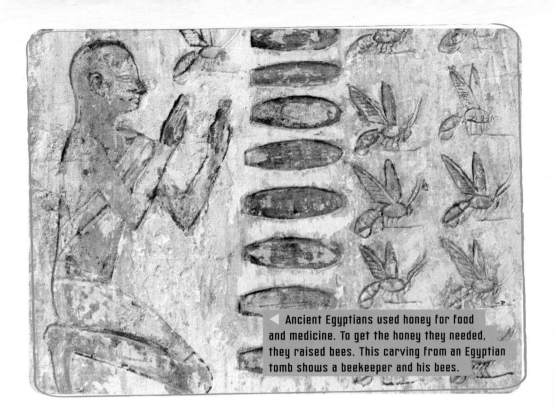

Ancient Egyptians used honey for food and medicine. To get the honey they needed, they raised bees. This carving from an Egyptian tomb shows a beekeeper and his bees.

Around 2500 B.C., Egyptians began raising their own bees. A stone carving on an Egyptian temple depicts the process. The carving shows beehives made from cylinders of dried mud. It shows people taking bees from the hives, removing honey, separating beeswax from honey, and storing honey in pottery jars.

WINE AND BEER

Wine and beer making were big business in ancient Egypt. At first ancient Egyptians imported wine from modern-day Lebanon and Israel. Then Egyptian farmers began to import grapevines from the same places, so they could grow their own grapes and make their own wine. Starting around 3000 B.C., Egyptian rulers oversaw large-scale wine-making operations. A wall painting from 1400 B.C. from the Egyptian city of Thebes (modern-day Luxor) shows two men picking grapes. Other men tread on a vat of grapes to make juice. The painting also shows amphorae, big containers for fermenting wine. The ancient Egyptians buried their kings in treasure-filled tombs. King

▲ Ancient Egyptians drank both wine and beer. This picture of ancient Egyptian wine making comes from the tomb of Ramses IX, who ruled Egypt in the 1100s B.C.

Tutankhamen, who died around 1352 B.C., was buried with twenty-six jugs of red and white wine, in addition to many other luxuries.

Egyptians did not drink beer just to quench their thirst or to get tipsy. Beer was a mainstay of the ancient Egyptian diet. Egyptian beer was thick and nutritious. It gave people healthful nutrients, such as calcium and potassium. Egyptians made beer from emmer wheat, the same grain used to make bread in ancient Egypt.

THE TOP FARMER

The United States has a Department of Agriculture. Its head is the U.S. secretary of agriculture. The ancient Egyptian government also had an agriculture department. The agency supervised irrigation, grain and livestock production, and relations between farmers and landlords. The head of Egypt's agriculture department was the grand vizier. Only the pharaoh, Egypt's chief ruler, had more power.

HOT STUFF

Spices were highly valued throughout the ancient world. Not only did spices enhance the flavor of foods, but they also masked the sour taste of food that had started to spoil. The ancient Egyptian queen Hatshepsut, who lived in the 1400s B.C., once sent traders to the mysterious land of Punt to buy spices. Scholars aren't sure where Punt was. It might have been modern-day Somalia in northeastern Africa.

Each area of the ancient world produced its own special spices. Ginger, cardamom, and pepper came from ancient India. Cinnamon came from Sri Lanka, an island south of India. Nutmeg and cloves came from islands in modern-day Indonesia, which were later nicknamed the Spice Islands.

Spices were costly in ancient times. In many places, only the nobility could afford them. Many ancient traders grew rich by buying and selling spices.

When it came time to pay taxes to the government, ancient Egyptians did not send money. They sent sacks full of nuts and grains to the vizier. They also sent livestock as taxes. The government stockpiled the extra food. If famine (widespread hunger) struck, the government used its stockpiles to feed hungry people.

ANCIENT CHINA

Mention food and China, and many people think of rice. Rice has long been an important crop in China. But it was not the first grain domesticated there. About nine thousand years ago, farmers in northern China domesticated millet. They then domesticated wheat, soybeans, barley, and other grains.

Rice cultivation (farming) in China began more than eight thousand years ago in the warm, moist Yangtze River valley. Wild rice grew throughout this area. Chinese hunter-gatherers gradually learned to save and plant rice seeds.

Because the soil in the Yangtze Valley was wet and heavy, ancient Chinese rice farmers needed sturdy tools. They used strong spades, or shovels, to dig into the soil. The spades had wooden handles and blades made from the shoulder bones of buffalo.

> "It was heavy, it was tall, it sprouted, it eared . . . it nodded, it hung . . . Indeed the lucky grains were sent down to us The black millet, the double-kernelled millet, pink-sprouted and white."
>
> —ancient Chinese poem, n.d.

PUDDLING RICE

The first Chinese farmers probably planted rice seeds directly into the soil, just as they planted other grains. But this approach posed problems. The rice seeds grew into mature plants, as expected. But weeds tended to

▼ This painting, made around A.D. 1700, shows off ancient Chinese agricultural technology in two different ways. First, the picture shows rice harvesting as it was done in ancient China. In addition, the painting is made on silk, a fabric first made in ancient China.

spring up along with the rice plants. So farmers needed to weed their fields often. In addition, rice plants need a lot of water. During wet years, Chinese rice crops flourished. But crops suffered during dry weather.

Around 800 B.C., Chinese farmers came up with a clever solution to both the weed problem and the water problem. They began to transplant rice seedlings (young rice plants) into paddies, or flooded fields. The process is called puddling, and it produced a better crop. In flooded fields, rice plants got plenty of water, even during dry spells. In addition, weeds couldn't grow in flooded fields.

Puddling improved the rice crop in ancient China, but it required specialized irrigation systems. Farmers had to build irrigation canals to carry water to their fields. They had to build barriers to keep water in the fields. They also built control gates to let water in and out of fields as necessary.

BIOLOGICAL PEST CONTROL

Worldwide, insects, fungi, rodents, and other pests destroy about 35 percent of all the crops people plant. Pests were a big problem for ancient farmers as well.

In modern times, farmers often use poisonous chemicals to kill insects and other pests on crops. In ancient China, farmers used a more natural method to kill insects. They used a system called biological pest control. Biological pest control involves killing pests with their own natural enemies. Often these enemies are other insects. For instance, praying mantises eat other bugs that can destroy plants. In ancient China, farmers released praying mantises into their flower and vegetable fields.

In some regions of ancient China, it was illegal to kill frogs. That's because frogs ate huge amounts of insects that damaged crops. Chinese fruit farmers hung burning torches in tree branches. The firelight attracted insects, which burned up when they reached the flames. Around A.D. 100, the Chinese began to use chrysanthemums, a type of flower, for biological pest control. Farmers dried the flowers and ground them into a fine powder. The powder killed insects on vegetable plants.

Some farmers in ancient China grew mandarin oranges. Like modern consumers, Chinese shoppers wanted flawless fruit for their money. They didn't want oranges damaged by fungus or filled with wormholes. Ancient Chinese fruit growers protected their oranges from pests with the help of yellow citrus killer ants. Growers released the ants into their orange trees. They sometimes built little bamboo bridges from tree to tree to help ants spread throughout the groves. In a book called *Records of the Plants and Trees of the Southern Regions*, a Chinese writer described the ants:

▲ Chrysanthemums contain chemicals that repel and kill some insects. Ancient Chinese farmers used the flowers to keep insects from eating their crops.

> The ants are reddish-yellow in color, bigger than ordinary
> ants. These ants do not eat the oranges, but attack and kill insects

which do. In the south, if the mandarin orange trees do not have this kind of ant, the fruits will be damaged by many harmful insects, and not a single fruit will be perfect.

MIXED-STOCK REARING

Fertilizer is a substance that enriches the soil. Animal manure is a natural and common fertilizer. Since ancient times, farmers have used manure from their own livestock to fertilize farmlands. Farmers in ancient China were no different.

Most ancient farmers raised a variety of crops and animals. For instance, ancient Chinese farmers often raised fish in ponds, kept livestock such as pigs, and grew fields of rice or other crops. Some ancient Chinese farmers took advantage of this variety to fertilize their rice fields. The farmers raised carp (a kind of fish) in ponds. They also kept pigs along the edges of the ponds. When it rained the pigs' manure washed into the ponds and settled at the bottom.

ANCIENT EATING UTENSILS: PART 2

People in China started using chopsticks *(right)* around 3000 B.C. Chopsticks allowed people to pick up hot pieces of food without burning their fingers. The first chopsticks were probably made from twigs. People later made chopsticks from bamboo stems, animal bones, animal tusks, and metal. From China, chopsticks spread to other parts of Asia.

▲ In this ancient Chinese stone carving, a man cuts up a fish with a knife. Another man hauls in a catch of fish, while more fish hang from a line.

After a while, the carp were grown and ready for market. The bottoms of the ponds were also filled with thick, well-fertilized soil. So farmers sold the carp and drained the ponds. Then they converted the empty ponds into puddled rice fields. Rice grew abundantly in the rich, manure-filled soil.

PEARL MAKERS

The raising of fish, shrimp, clams, and other water animals is called aquaculture. Farmers mostly practice aquaculture to produce food. But one kind of aquaculture produces valuable gems. The gems are pearls.

Pearls come from oysters, a type of shellfish. An oyster will create a pearl when a foreign substance, such as a bit of sand, enters its shell. The foreign material irritates the oyster, much as a piece of dirt can irritate a person's eye. In response to the irritation, the oyster secretes layers of nacre, or mother-of-pearl. This shiny material coats the irritant. The nacre also hardens to become a pearl.

The ancient Chinese were the first pearl farmers. First, they simply collected pearls that grew naturally in oysters. To get more pearls, the ancient Chinese began deliberately putting sand and other material into oysters' shells. Pearls made deliberately instead of naturally are called cultured pearls.

People in the ancient world valued pearls just as modern people do. Wealthy women wanted to wear pearl earrings and necklaces. Chinese merchants made a lot of money by selling pearls to people in other ancient lands.

DOMESTICATING A WORM

The ancient Chinese raised many kinds of farm animals. Some Chinese farmers even raised insects. These insects were silkworms. Silkworms give us silk fabric. People have long prized this fabric for its shimmery beauty. Silk is extremely strong but also lightweight.

Silkworms change form as they grow to be adults. They turn from worms into moths. During the growing process, silkworms spin outer wrappings called cocoons. Cocoons are made of long silk fibers. In a few weeks after completing their cocoons, the silkworms turn into full-grown moths. Then the moths burst out of their cocoons. In the process, they break the long silk fibers into short ones.

People in ancient China wanted long silk fibers to make silk fabric. They developed a technique to get silk fibers from cocoons before silkworm moths could break them. First, silkworm farmers collected the

▲ Silk making hasn't changed much since ancient times. In this modern photograph, silkworms crawl on mulberry leaves, their primary source of food. Soon these worms will wrap themselves in silk cocoons.

eggs of silkworm moths. They kept the eggs warm until they hatched into tiny silkworms. Farmers fed the young silkworms the chopped-up leaves of mulberry trees. After four or five weeks, the silkworms spun their cocoons on twigs or pieces of straw. Before the silkworm moths could burst out of their cocoons, farmers heated the cocoons in ovens to kill the insects inside. Silk farmers then boiled the cocoons to remove the sticky substance holding the silk in place. They unwound the silk from the cocoons and twisted together silk strands to form thread. The silk thread was then woven into fabric. Modern silkworm farmers still use this process.

▲ This ancient Chinese blanket dates to the fourth or fifth century B.C. The blanket was made with pricey materials, including silk, gold, and leather.

Each silkworm cocoon contains only a small amount of silk. In fact, it takes about twenty-seven hundred silkworms to make 1 pound (0.5 kg) of silk fabric. Thus silk is expensive. In ancient Rome, silk fabric cost as much as an equal weight of gold.

According to legend, the wife of an ancient Chinese emperor discovered silkworm cocoons around 2700 B.C. She then started the first silkworm farm. Once they had learned to make silk, the ancient Chinese kept the process a carefully guarded secret. Since no one outside China knew how to make silk, people in other countries had to buy their silk from China.

Chinese merchants sold silk to traders in other countries. In turn, traders carried goods from Europe and the Middle East to China. The traders traveled along a series of roads that linked China, India, central Asia, and the Middle East. In addition to silk, traders carried spices, pearls, cotton, precious stones, incense, and other goods. But because silk was such a bigger seller, the series of trade routes became known as the Silk Road.

Around A.D. 300, people in Japan and India discovered the secret to silk making and began producing their own silk. But people farther west still didn't know how to make it. They continued to pay high prices for silk from the East. In about 550, Justinian I, head of the Byzantine (Eastern Roman) Empire, sent two monks on a spying mission to China. The monks learned the secret of silk making. They stole mulberry seeds and silkworm eggs, hid them inside their walking staffs, and brought them back to Constantinople (modern-day Istanbul, Turkey). From Constantinople, silk-making technology spread to Europe.

▼ Merchants carried silk, incense, and many more products along the Silk Road, a series of trade routes between China and the Middle East. Two thousand years ago, the city of Gaochang in northern China was a stop on the road. In modern times, all that remains of the city are the bases of old stone buildings.

ANCIENT ICE CREAM

Food historians don't know who made the first ice cream. The ancient Chinese might have been the inventors. Starting about 700 B.C., the Chinese made a frozen mixture of milk, cream, honey, and other ingredients. The people who made the ice cream probably used a simple technique. They put the ingredients inside a small container. They placed that container into a larger container filled with ice, snow, and saltpeter (a kind of mineral). The saltpeter made the ice and snow even colder, thereby freezing the ingredients in the inner container. The final product probably resembled modern-day sherbet.

Ancient peoples also poured fruit, juices, honey, or sugar over snow or ice to make a dessert much like modern-day snow cones or Italian ices. Food historians say that the ancient Greek general Alexander the Great and the ancient Roman emperor Nero both loved such flavored ices.

TEATIME

Tea is made by pouring boiling water over the dried leaves of the tea plant. Legend says an ancient Chinese emperor made the first tea in 2737 B.C., when leaves from a tea plant accidentally fell into a pot of boiling water.

Whatever its origins, tea drinking spread throughout China and then to other parts of ancient Asia. At first ancient peoples drank tea as medicine. Eventually, people began drinking tea for its stimulant effects. Like coffee, tea contains caffeine. This chemical stimulates the nervous system, making people feel more awake and alert.

THE ANCIENT AMERICAS

People first came to the Americas about fifteen thousand years ago—perhaps earlier. They came from Siberia in northeastern Asia. In modern times, the Pacific Ocean completely separates Asia and the Americas. But thousands of years ago, a bridge of land linked Siberia and modern-day Alaska. Anthropologists think that ancient Siberians walked over this bridge to North America. But some might have walked over thick ice near the bridge or taken boats over open stretches of ocean. These newcomers were hunter-gatherers. They probably followed herds of animals into North America.

▲ In ancient Aztec culture, Yacatecuhtli was the god of trade. In this painting, he carries maize, or corn, in his hand, on his back, and on his head. Corn was an important food for people throughout much of the ancient Americas.

Ancient Americans then moved south through modern-day Canada, onto the American Great Plains, and into modern-day Mexico and Central America. They reached the tip of South America in about 9000 B.C. Different groups encountered different environments as they migrated south, and separate cultures developed.

FOOD FIRST

The ancient Americans left little written information about their food and agriculture. But they did leave some agricultural artifacts (physical remains), such as grinding stones, irrigation ditches, spindles for spinning wool, and vessels for holding food. Some ancient American artists made pictures and sculptures of corn gods and other deities. People probably gave gifts and said prayers to these gods in hopes of a good harvest. Some ancient American artwork shows people harvesting crops and preparing foods. In the late 1400s, European explorers began to arrive in the Americas. They wrote extensively about the peoples they encountered. Some of these writings tell us about ancient American agriculture.

Experts think that ancient Americans first began to grow crops eight to ten thousand years ago. In Mexico people domesticated corn (also called maize), squash, and beans. In the Andes Mountains of South America, people domesticated beans, potatoes, and a grain called quinoa.

As in the ancient Middle East, the growth of agriculture in ancient America led to other changes in society. When ancient Americans settled down and began to grow crops, they also built villages. Some villages became big cities. Eventually, complex civilizations emerged in the ancient Americas. Mexico and Central America were home to a series of ancient civilizations—first the Maya, then the Toltec, and then the Aztecs. In South America, people called the Inca developed a powerful empire.

North America did not have powerful ancient empires such as the Inca or the Maya. Why not? Perhaps because most people there did not settle down into farming villages. So they did not go on to build big cities or big empires. Most ancient North Americans live in small family groups. They got their food by hunting and gathering. However, some ancient North Americans did take up farming, which they used in combination with hunting and gathering. A few North American groups, such as the Pueblos of the present-day U.S. Southwest, were primarily farmers. Like peoples in ancient Mexico and Central America, they mostly grew corn, squash, and beans.

BEANS WITH BAD VALVES

Domesticating plants is much like domesticating animals. People choose plants with the most desirable traits, gather their seeds, and plant them to perpetuate the desirable traits in the next generation of plants. Over time, domesticated plants become very different from their wild ancestors.

The story of domesticated beans shows this process in action. The modern-day common bean, with the scientific name *Phaseolus vulgaris*, comes in many varieties. These include black beans, kidney beans, and pinto beans. All these beans have a common wild ancestor. It grew in ancient South and Central America.

▼ These modern-day red common beans are very different from their wild bean ancestors. Wild beans split open easily, making it hard for people to collect their seeds. Domesticated beans don't split easily. Their seeds stay in the pods.

This wild plant frustrated the American farmers. When a wild bean plant matured, its pods opened. Each pod split into two valves, or halves, and ejected edible seeds. This system was good for the bean. It was nature's way of spreading bean seeds and making sure they grew into new plants each season. But the system was inefficient for ancient Americans. Seeds often shot out of bean pods before anyone could collect them. If ancient Americans wanted to grow beans, they had to collect pods with "bad valves." Those were pods that didn't split easily or didn't split at all.

Ancient American farmers collected these pods and saved the beans for planting. Many of the beans grew into plants that also had bad valves. Their seeds stayed in the bean pods until harvesttime. Then people collected the pods and opened them to collect the beans. This practice of harvesting and planting beans with bad pod valves eventually gave us modern common beans.

MAYAN FARMERS

From about 400 B.C. to A.D. 900, the Maya lived in Central America and southern Mexico. To clear lands for farming, Mayans used a technique called slash-and-burn agriculture. Using stone axes, they chopped down trees in a section of forest. After the wood dried out, the farmers set the field on fire. Burning not only cleared the land. It also left a layer of ash on the soil. The ash provided nutrients for crops.

▼ Slash-and-burn agriculture is an ancient technology that is still used in some parts of the world. Here, people in Brazil have burned down trees to clear a field. They will plant crops on the cleared land.

On their newly cleared land, Mayan farmers planted corn, beans, and squash. After a few years of planting, the soil in the field began to grow less fertile. So farmers moved on to slash, burn, and plant another area of forest.

Central America and southern Mexico have a wet season from June to October and a dry season from November to May. During the wet season, rain often falls daily. Ancient Mayan farmers needed to save some rainwater from the wet season for use during the dry season. They collected rainwater in ditches and other natural reservoirs (storage ponds). They also built irrigation channels and small dams, which helped them move water to and from reservoirs. Where the land was swampy, Mayan farmers dug drainage ditches to dry it out.

After digging irrigation ditches, the Maya sometimes piled the dug-up soil between two ditches. They grew crops on top of the piles. They also dredged nutrient-rich muck from the bottom of the irrigation ditches and used it as fertilizer. Mayan farmers mulched (covered) crops with layers of leaves. The mulch helped keep the soil from drying out.

Modern farmers use a technique called crop rotation, which involves planting fields with different crops from year to year. Some crops, such as corn, take nitrogen from the soil. Other crops, such as beans, add nitrogen to the soil. If a farmer plants corn in the same field year after year, soon all the nitrogen will be used up and the corn won't

People in many ancient cultures prayed to food gods, asking for a good harvest. This sculpture depicts the Mayan corn god. It comes from the palace of Yax Pac, a Mayan king, and dates to around A.D. 775.

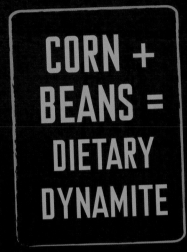

CORN + BEANS = DIETARY DYNAMITE

The Maya knew that corn and beans grew well together. The Maya also often ate corn and beans together in one meal. In doing so, they happened upon a nearly perfect food combination. Both beans and corn are healthful foods on their own. But neither contains the full variety of amino acids that the human body needs. Amino acids are essential to good health. Corn is low in an amino acid called lysine but is especially rich in another amino acid, methionine. Beans are rich in lysine but low in methionine. Eaten together, beans and corn provide the body with its full assortment of amino acids.

grow well. By rotating crops and beans from year to year, however, the soil stays fertile. Mayan farmers used a variation on crop rotation. They planted corn and beans in the same fields. That way, the beans restored the nitrogen that the corn plants removed. Mayan farmers also planted squash among the corn and beans.

GUM AND CHOCOLATE

Sapodilla trees grow wild in the forests of Mexico and Central America. They produce a delicious brown fruit that tastes like pears. They also produce a milky sap called chicle. If you boil chicle to remove the water, you're left with a thick, tasteless, gummy substance. The Maya chewed chicle. It was the world's first chewing gum.

SOMETHING TO CHEW ON

▲ Chicle comes from the sap of the sapodilla tree, shown here with fruit hanging off the tree's branches.

Long after the end of Mayan culture, people in Mexico and Central America continued to chew chicle. But the chewy substance was unknown in other parts of the world. In the 1860s, U.S. inventor Thomas Adams obtained some chicle from Mexico. He wanted to use it to make rubber, but he couldn't make that work. Then Adams tried chewing the stuff. He realized that with some sugar and flavoring, chicle would make an enjoyable confection.

Adams began selling chicle-based chewing gum. The U.S. public loved it. Soon other companies wanted a piece of the chewing gum action. Adams and other manufacturers sent people deep into the rain forests of Central America to gather chicle. One early brand of chewing gum was called Chiclets, named for chicle. In the 1940s, chewing gum manufacturers stopped using chicle. They switched to easier-to-obtain synthetic (human-made) substances as a base for chewing gum.

The Maya were also the first people to consume chocolate. Chocolate comes from the beans of cacao trees, which grow wild in Mexico and Central America. The Maya made a chocolate drink. They roasted and ground cacao beans and mixed them with mashed corn, water, hot chili peppers, and spices. The drink was served at room temperature and was not sweetened. It probably tasted bitter.

> ## "Every now and then was handed to him a golden pitcher filled with a kind of liquor made from the cacao, which is of a very exciting nature."

—Bernal Díaz Del Castillo, Spanish soldier and historian, describing a chocolate drink, 1632

AGRICULTURE IN THE ANDES

The Andes Mountains of South America were home to many different ancient peoples. Like other ancient Americans, the peoples of the Andes started out as hunter-gatherers and later became farmers. In the process, they domesticated plants and animals.

Ancient Andean hunters killed wild animals called guanacos and vicuñas. Both are related to camels. Gradually, ancient Andean people domesticated both animals. Guanacos became llamas. These long-eared animals stand 3 to 4 feet (0.9 to 1.2 m) high at the shoulder. They have long, thick wool. Andean farmers used male llamas to carry heavy loads. Farmers raised

▼ Llamas *(below)* are domesticated animals related to camels. Their wild ancestors are called guanacos. Ancient Andean people raised llamas for milk, meat, and wool. Male llamas also carried heavy loads on their backs.

females for meat and milk. Farmers used the wool and skins from both males and females to make cloth and leather. Meanwhile, vicuñas became modern alpacas. Alpacas are smaller than llamas. Ancient Andeans raised these animals mainly for their long wool, which is silkier and straighter than sheep's wool. Ancient Andeans herded and bred llamas and alpacas much as other ancient peoples herded and bred goats and sheep.

Archaeologists think that ancient Andeans also domesticated guinea pigs. Guinea pigs have tasty meat, and ancient Andeans raised them for food. Archaeologists have found guinea pig bones at the site of ancient settlements in Peru, Ecuador, and Argentina. Guinea pigs were probably easy to domesticate. They reproduce rapidly, eat household scraps, and can be raised in pens. Guinea pigs are attracted to the warmth and garbage of human

▼ By cutting terraces into hillsides, ancient and modern farmers can create flat growing surfaces. The terraces below were cut by ancient farmers in the Incan city of Machu Picchu in what is now Peru.

settlements. Ancient Andeans might have discovered nests of guinea pigs in the corners of their huts and then began breeding the animals.

Andean farmers raised a variety of crops, including corn, beans, peanuts, and quinoa. Archaeologists think that ancient people in Bolivia first domesticated potatoes around 5000 B.C.

The Incas were skilled farmers. They built irrigation canals to bring water to dry areas. In hilly areas, Incan farmers cut terraces into the slopes. The terraces gave farmers flat surfaces for planting crops. Terraces also helped keep soil from washing away during rainstorms.

ANCIENT GREECE

▲ In ancient Greece in the second century A.D., a man named Oppianus wrote a poem about fishing. About one thousand years later, someone put the text into a book. This drawing of Greek fishermen accompanies the text.

Ancient Greek civilization flourished from about 500 to 146 B.C. During this time, the ancient Greeks made lasting contributions to science, art, and philosophy. Greek architects designed imposing temples and other public buildings. Greek playwrights penned thought-provoking tragedies and comedies. Ancient Greek city-states established the world's first democratic governments. But along with these lofty pursuits, the ancient Greeks still had to attend to basic needs. Like people in every society, they needed systems for raising, processing, and distributing food.

Greece is mostly surrounded by water. The Aegean Sea sits to the east of Greece. The Ionian Sea is to the west. The Sea of Crete is to the south. All of these waters are arms of the Mediterranean Sea, which also lies south of Greece. Much of Greece is made up of large and small islands. With so much water all around them, the ancient Greeks naturally looked to the surrounding seas for food. They ate lots of fish and shellfish.

The ancient Greeks were also farmers. But Greece is rugged, rocky, and hilly. Much of the land is not good for farming. Where the land was suitable, the ancient Greeks built small farms. But farming and fishing alone could not produce enough food for the population. So the ancient Greeks imported a lot of food from neighboring lands.

ANCIENT EATING UTENSILS: PART 3

The ancient Greeks did not use knives or spoons as eating utensils. Instead, they ate with their fingers. They liked their meals served scalding hot and often burned their fingers while eating hot foods. One Greek gourmet, Philoxenus, trained himself to withstand the heat. He prepared his fingers by dipping them in hot water. He drank hot water to prepare his mouth and throat for the hottest morsels of food.

The ancient Greeks used big forks for carving and serving meat, but they didn't use small forks at the dinner table. People in ancient Turkey and the Middle East were the first ones to use small forks as eating utensils.

OIL AND WINE

Olives and grapes grew wild in ancient Greece. At first Greek farmers simply gathered the wild fruits. Farmers crushed the olives to make olive oil. They crushed the grapes to make wine. In the 700s B.C., Greek farmers started to domesticate olive trees. They collected seeds from the wild trees that yielded the most oil, knowing that the offspring of these trees would also be good oil producers. Greek farmers also domesticated grapes.

To process these fruits, Greek farmers used a machine called a screw press. The screw press used the power of a large turning screw to crush grapes or olives inside a container. Sometimes oxen turned the big screw. Sometimes a single laborer did the work.

LAERTES' FARM

The Odyssey is a long poem by Homer, an ancient Greek writer. Written around 700 B.C., *The Odyssey* features a hero named Ulysses. Ulysses tries to return home to the Greek island of Ithaca after the Trojan War (which might have taken place around 1200 B.C.). Along the way, he has many adventures.

Ulysses wants to return to the farm of his father, Laertes. Homer's description of Laertes' farm tells us a lot about agriculture in ancient Greece. On Laertes' farm, Homer writes, "Everything is well cared for, and there is never a plant, neither fig tree nor grapevine nor olive nor pear tree nor leek bed uncared for."

Homer says that Laertes fertilized the soil with manure and irrigated his fields. He raised a variety of crops that kept him and his workers busy all

> ## "There is the place where his fruit trees are grown tall and flourish, pear trees and pomegranate trees and the flourishing olive."
>
> —Homer, *The Odyssey*, 700s B.C.

year. They reaped and threshed wheat and barley in early summer. They picked pears, figs, and other fruit in June, July, and August. In August and September, they harvested grapes and produced wine. Then they planted the next season's wheat. In between all these activities, the workers picked vegetables, ground grain into flour, and attended to other farm chores.

IRRIGATION SYSTEMS

Fruit trees and grapevines need a lot of water. They must be irrigated for several years after planting, until they grow strong roots. In Greece, irrigation is especially important during the hot summer months.

Greece has no big river like the Nile in Egypt to provide water for large irrigation projects. So farmers in ancient Greece relied on small irrigation systems. They dammed and diverted streams and springs to bring water to their fields. They hoisted water from wells and poured it into storage tanks or irrigation channels.

Ancient Greek farmers used shadoofs to move water more easily. Another helpful device was the *saqiya*, invented in ancient Persia (modern-day Iran). This machine consisted of a series of buckets attached to a rope, which was connected to two large interlocking wooden wheels. An ox turned one of the wheels. This wheel turned the second wheel, which lifted the chain of buckets from a well. The machine brought bucket after bucket of water to the top of the well, where the water could be dumped into a tank or irrigation channel.

In the 200s B.C., the Greek engineer Archimedes of Syracuse made an even better water-hoisting machine. This device was called an Archimedes' screw.

It was a hollow tube with a big screw inside. The bottom of the tube sat in the water. With the device propped at about a 45-degree angle, a worker turned a crank to operate the screw. As the crank rotated, water trapped in the threads of the screw rose higher and higher until it spilled out of the top of the tube.

MILLING GRAIN

One sound could be heard throughout the day in most ancient households. It was the constant grating sound of people grinding grain by hand. Ancient people did this job with the help of mortars, pestles, and querns. A mortar is a small stone bowl or tray for holding kernels of grain. A pestle is a narrow stone tool used for crushing grain inside a mortar. A quern is a flat stone that holds kernels to be crushed with a roller. In ancient times, one person working all day with such tools could grind only enough flour to feed a few people. In a large household, several people had to work all day on the task.

WONDER BREAD

The Greeks were the master bakers of the ancient world. They made bread from different kinds of flour, including wheat, barley, and rye flour. Athenaeus, a Greek writer who lived around A.D. 200, compiled a list of more than seventy different kinds of bread made in ancient Greece. In addition to bread, ancient Greek bakeries sold cakes and pastries made with oat flour, honey, cream, dried fruits, and nuts. The ancient Greeks even made cheesecake.

The job usually fell to the women of the family.

The sounds of grinding grain by hand began to disappear in ancient Greece around 100 B.C.. That's when professional millers took over the job. People brought their grain to millers, who charged a fee for turning it into flour.

Instead of working with handheld mortars and pestles, millers placed large amounts of grain between big flat stones called millstones. Some stones were 2 or 3 feet (0.6 to 0.9 m) wide. Big wooden spokes projected from the stones. Slaves or animals turned the stones by walking in a circle. Some Greek mills operated on water power. Their millstones were attached to a waterwheel, which sat in a river and turned with the current. A commercial mill could grind more grain in an hour than several people with hand tools could do in a whole day.

CHAPTER SEVEN

ANCIENT ROME

▲ This mosaic (a picture made with colored stones or tiles) comes from ancient Rome and dates to the fourth century A.D. The mosaic shows Romans harvesting grapes for making wine.

Nomadic people called the Latins started grazing herds of sheep in central Italy around 2000 B.C. By 750 B.C., the Latins had settled into permanent farming villages. One village grew into the city of Rome. The Romans conquered other groups on the Italian Peninsula. They established a republic, a government with elected officials, in 509 B.C. In the first century B.C., Roman leaders fought among themselves for power. In 27 B.C., a nobleman named Octavian took complete control of the Roman government. He declared himself emperor of Rome. Eventually, the Roman Empire conquered vast amounts of territory, from Europe to northern Africa to the Middle East.

These circles of stone near Rome are all that remain of ancient grain containers. In ancient times, people filled the containers with grain to be ground into flour.

ROMAN FARMERS

The Italian Peninsula has fertile farmland along its many river valleys. Ancient Roman farmers grew olives, grapes, wheat, and other fruits and vegetables. They used tools, seeds, and techniques created earlier throughout the Mediterranean world. These included irrigation systems and ox-drawn plows.

Roman farmers also developed agricultural techniques of their own. For instance, they left half of every field fallow, or unplanted, each year. The soil in this uncultivated land stored up nutrients from decayed plant matter and animal droppings. It stored up moisture from rain and humidity. The soil became more fertile for the next time it was planted. The Romans also rotated crops from field to field. One year they would plant wheat, which robbed the soil of nitrogen. The next year, they would plant legumes, such as beans, which restored nitrogen and enriched the soil.

NEW MACHINES

Reaping is the process of cutting stalks of wheat and other grains at harvesttime. Throughout the ancient world, farmers used scythes for reaping.

A scythe has a long curved blade and a long wooden handle. Reaping grain with a scythe is slow, hard work.

In the first century A.D., farmers in the Roman Empire area known as Gaul (modern-day France and Belgium) devised a machine to make reaping easier. It was called a *vallus*. The machine was a two-wheeled, boxlike cart with one end open. The box contained a row of sharp metal blades. A donkey pushed the cart forward through a field of grain, while a laborer steered the cart and directed the stalks into the blades. When the blades cut the stalks, the grain fell into the cart. The vallus saved a lot of labor. Pliny the Elder, a Roman writer, described the machine: "On the vast estates in the provinces of Gaul very large frames fitted with teeth at the edge and carried on two wheels are driven through the corn [grain] by a donkey pushing from behind; the ears torn off fall into the frame." Ancient Romans also built a larger version of the vallus, called a *carpentum*.

FISH FARMING

Many ancient peoples, including the Egyptians, Chinese, and Japanese, practiced aquaculture (water-based farming). But some the biggest and most elaborate ancient fish farms were in ancient Rome. One big fish farm was located at Cosa, a port city north of the city of Rome. The farm produced about 3 million pounds (1.4 million kg) of fish each year. The fish lived in concrete tanks filled with seawater. The farm covered 2.5 acres (1 hectare) of land.

The ancient Roman city of Cosa stands in ruins in modern times. In ancient times, Cosa was a thriving port city with a big fish farm.

The Romans bred only the largest fish, knowing that the offspring of large fish would probably also be large. They even fed fish high-calorie foods enriched with olive oil and wine. One Roman oyster farm, built around 100 B.C., used heated water, which made oysters grow more quickly.

DINNERTIME

Most ordinary Romans ate a simple diet. Staple foods included bread, olives, mashed beans, chickpeas, wine, cheese, salted fish, and small amounts of poultry and red meat. For a special treat, Romans ate wheat cakes dipped in honey or milk. Another taste treat was porridge made from bread crumbs and onions fried in olive oil.

Rich Romans, on the other hand, liked to live large. They held lavish banquets and feasted until they were stuffed. The wealthy dined on rare and expensive fishes and meats.

▲ Wealthy ancient Romans loved to drink and dine. This wall painting from the city of Pompeii shows wealthy Romans at a banquet. They recline while servants attend them.

Marcus Gavius Apicius, a first-century Roman gourmet (food lover), traveled throughout the empire and racked up large debts to satisfy his taste for fine foods. He documented some of the ancient Rome's most elaborate recipes in a book called *The Art of Cooking*. Here Apicius gives a recipe for boiled ostrich:

> Pepper, mint, roast cumin, celery seed, dates or Jericho dates, honey, vinegar, passum [dessert wine], garum [fish paste], a little oil. Put these in the pot and bring to the boil. Bind with amulum [starch], pour over the pieces of ostrich in a serving dish and sprinkle with pepper. If you wish to cook the ostrich in the sauce, add alica [spelt].

"Our minds are like our stomachs; they are whetted [stimulated] by the change of their food, and variety supplies both with fresh appetite."

—Marcus Fabius Quintilian, Roman orator, first century A.D.

SPICES

The ancient craving for spices reached its peak in the Roman Empire. An entire section of the city of Rome, the Spice Quarter, was devoted to the buying and selling of cloves, ginger, nutmeg, black and white pepper, cinnamon, turmeric, and other spices. Wealthy Romans used these spices liberally to enhance the taste of food.

Merchants in the Spice Quarter also bought and sold camphor, sandalwood, frankincense, myrrh, and balsam. These substances are fragrant plant by-products. People used them not as food but as incense, perfume, and sometimes medicine.

Garum was a widely used condiment in ancient Rome. Garum was a paste made from fish intestines and olive oil. Ancient Romans used it to liven up everything from eggs to meats to stews.

▲ In the ancient city of Rome, people could buy foods and spices from around the ancient world. This stone carving shows a buyer and a seller at a market stall. The carving dates to the early part of the first millennium A.D.

AND ICES

The Romans loved to eat flavored and sweetened ices for dessert. They also loved iced drinks. They cooled wine and fruit juices before drinking them. The ancient Roman drink cooler worked just like a modern ice bucket.

SALT OF THE EARTH

For good health, humans and other animals need to eat small quantities of sodium chloride, or salt, each day. Modern people tend to eat too much salt, especially in prepared foods and snacks. Too much salt can lead to high blood pressure. It's not uncommon to see foods labeled "salt-free" and "low-salt" on modern supermarket shelves.

Thousands of years ago, however, people did not try to avoid salt. In fact, they devoted great amounts of time and effort to getting the salt they needed. Ancient peoples not only ate salted foods but also used salt to process and preserve foods. Salt kept fish and meat from spoiling. It was used to make cheese, pickled vegetables, and other foods. Farmers fed salt to their livestock.

Salt comes from underground deposits, and many places were named for the salt that was mined or processed there. For instance, the place-name Salzburg (a city in Austria) means "salt town" in German. *Hals* is the ancient Greek word for salt, and the cities of Halle, Belgium, and Halluin, France, were both named for their saltworks—or salt-processing facilities.

Some ancient trading routes were called salt roads. Traders traveled along these roads with blocks of salt carried on the backs of camels, donkeys, and mules. One salt road extended from salt deposits in modern-day Ethiopia to markets in ancient Egypt and Rome. At markets, merchants sold salt in blocks, lumps, cakes, and sheets.

Salt was so important that ancient peoples even used pieces of salt as money. The ancient Roman government paid soldiers partly in salt. The payment was called a *salarium* (*sal* is the Latin word for "salt"). That's the origin of our modern word *salary*, which means "a worker's pay." You might have heard someone remark, "He's not worth his salt." That's another way of saying, "He's not worth the money they pay him."

Ancient peoples fought over salt. Countries sometimes went to war for control of salt mines. Pirates often raided ships carrying salt, and robbers stole shipments of salt along trading routes.

The cooler consisted of two pottery jars, one inside the other. The inner jar held wine or another beverage. The outer jar held ice or snow, which cooled the contents of the inner jar. Romans also put chips of ice and scoops of snow into their glasses to keep drinks chilled.

The Romans also used ice for cold baths in summer, to preserve fish, and to keep other food from spoiling. But Italy and many other parts of the Roman Empire were warm places, without much snowy weather. Where did the ancient Romans get snow and ice? They transported it on the backs of mules from snow-covered mountain peaks. When ice merchants reached the city, they sold some of the supply to snow and ice shops, which sold to consumers.

Some of the ice went into storage in icehouses. These were underground pits, sometimes more than 30 feet (9 m) deep. The cool underground temperatures helped keep the ice from melting. A layer of straw, grass, or leaves sealed the pit opening and served as insulation. It kept cool air inside the pit and warm air out. Ice kept in underground pits would stay frozen for many months.

AFTER THE ANCIENTS

Ancient societies rose and fell. Often ancient groups grew politically or economically weak and stronger groups conquered them. But even after an ancient culture died out, its technology often remained. Conquering groups built on the knowledge of conquered peoples to further develop technology.

The Roman Empire fell to invaders in A.D. 476. After that, Europe entered a period called the Middle Ages (about 500 to 1500). The Middle Ages are sometimes called the Dark Ages, because art, culture, and learning were minimal in Europe during these years. Few people in Europe went to school. Few craftspeople knew about or improved upon ancient technology.

But farming technology was a bright spot during the Middle Ages. In Europe, farmers continued to improve on agricultural techniques developed by ancient peoples. For instance, European farmers developed a three-field system of crop rotation. They left one field fallow each year and grew different crops on the other two. This system restored nutrients to the soil but also kept plenty of land under cultivation. European farmers also figured out how to hitch horses to plows during the Middle Ages. Horses could pull plows much faster than oxen could, so they enabled European farmers to plow more land, plant more seeds, and grow more food. European farmers also continued to breed plants and livestock to produce desirable traits in their offspring. Farmers in northwestern France bred Guernsey cows, which produce a lot of butterfat-rich milk. People use butterfat to make butter.

During the Middle Ages, European farmers improved some tools and techniques. But they continued to cut grain by hand, as illustrated in this religious book from Norway, created in about A.D. 1230.

EXPANDING FOOD HORIZONS

In the 1300s, Europe entered an era called the Renaissance. This was a time of renewed interest in art, learning, and culture. Europeans also began to explore lands beyond their borders during the Renaissance. In 1492 Italian explorer Christopher Columbus set out across the Atlantic Ocean by ship. He believed that by sailing west around the world, he would reach the Pacific Ocean and Asia.

Columbus was right. It was possible to reach Asia by sailing west from Europe. But Columbus didn't realize that a huge landmass sat between the Atlantic and Pacific oceans. That landmass consisted of North, Central, and South America. Columbus had discovered what Europeans called a New World. Of course, the land was not new to the millions of ancient Americans who called it home.

After Columbus, more European explorers visited the Americas. Settlers and soldiers also arrived to claim various American territories for Spain, France, England, Holland, and other European nations. The newcomers arrived in America hoping to find gold, silver, and other riches—and some of them did. But the Europeans also found something unexpected. They discovered a host of foods unknown in Europe. These foods included corn, potatoes, chili peppers, tomatoes, pineapples, peanuts, chocolate, vanilla beans, and avocados.

Merchants began to ship some of these foods back to Europe, where consumers were excited by the new taste treats. Europeans didn't like the bitter-tasting chocolate drink from Central America. By when they added sugar to the mixture and heated it, a new taste sensation—hot chocolate—was born. European farmers found that certain American foods, such as tomatoes and potatoes, grew well in Europe. Other American foods, such as pineapples, grew only in warm, wet tropical places. To obtain more of these foods, European planters began to grow them in their tropical colonies in Asia, Africa, and America.

Ancient Americans also introduced European explorers and settlers to tobacco. Americans grew this plant extensively and enjoyed smoking it. The product caught on quickly in Europe, especially since it is addictive. Some European farmers began to grow tobacco, but the best tobacco came from Virginia in the present-day United States. In the early 1600s, an English colonist named John Rolfe began growing tobacco in Virginia and shipping it to England.

BIG LEAPS FORWARD

For thousands of years, farmers did most of their work by hand. At planting time, they walked along their furrows, scattering seeds of grain. At harvesttime, they cut grain with scythes. Farmers had animals to help them, but they had little mechanical equipment.

That changed in the 1700s. In that century, inventors began to build mechanized farm equipment. An Englishman named Jethro Tull invented a mechanical seed drill. This machine dug small trenches in soil and deposited seeds in the trenches. The machine replaced the earlier technique of scattering seeds by hand. The drill ensured that seeds ended up right where farmers wanted them, and it cut down on wasted and unevenly planted seeds.

▼ British painter John Nost Sartorius, who lived from 1759 to 1828, painted this English harvest scene. Hand labor was replaced by mechanized tools in the Western world, starting in the 1700s.

▲ Cyrus McCormick's reaper *(above)*, invented in the 1830s, was similar to the ancient Roman vallus. The reaper cut stalks of grain mechanically. People no longer had to use scythes and sickles to cut grain by hand.

In the United States, Eli Whitney invented the cotton gin in 1793. This machine separated cotton fibers from cotton seeds. It enabled farmers to grow large amounts of cotton, which became a leading crop in the United States. Another important invention was the mechanical reaper. Built by American Cyrus McCormick in the 1830s, the reaper cut off grain stocks at harvesttime much like the vallus had in ancient Rome. In 1837 American John Deere invented the steel plow. This plow turned the soil much more easily and cleanly than earlier iron or wooden plows.

PICKING UP STEAM

Farmers continued to use horses, oxen, and other animals to power their farm equipment. But that changed in the 1890s, with the arrival of gasoline power. In the United States, Europe, and other wealthy areas, farmers began to use gasoline-powered tractors to pull plows, reapers, and other farm machinery. In the twentieth century, farms became more and more mechanized. Farmers

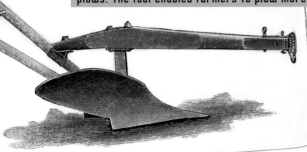

John Deere's steel plow cut through soil more easily than earlier wooden or iron plows. The tool enabled farmers to plow more land and grow more food.

bought electric cow-milking machines and electric irrigation pumps. Agricultural companies developed new chemical fertilizers, insecticides, and weed killers. The breeding of plants and animals became more and more specialized and scientific.

By the mid-1900s, farming had become big business in the United States and other countries. Big corporations set up giant farming operations covering hundreds of thousands of acres of land. These agribusinesses borrowed techniques from factories to make their farming operations more efficient. Some big farms focused on growing a single crop, such as corn. Others raised pigs, chickens, or other livestock in special buildings. Farm managers gave animals drugs to keep them healthy and to make them grow larger.

This modern gasoline-powered machine is a combine, or combined harvester-thresher. It cuts stalks of wheat, separates the wheat kernels from the rest of the stalks, and deposits the kernels in a container truck.

THE BIGGEST AND THE BEST?

At first glance, agribusiness seems to have paid off for the United States. In the twenty-first century, U.S. food supplies seem endless. Agribusinesses produce vast amounts of crops and raise millions of animals. At U.S. supermarkets, consumers can choose from a dizzying array of fruits, vegetables, meats, fish, dairy products, and packaged foods. The results of modern agribusiness are impressive.

But to many people, the results of modern agribusiness are also troubling. Chemical fertilizers help improve farm yields. But they can also pollute lakes and rivers. Chemical insecticides are effective in killing bugs that harm crops. But they can also leave poisonous residues on plants. The drug and chemicals that make farm animals grow large and meaty might also damage the health

Some consumers want only organic fruits and vegetables, which are grown without chemical pesticides. More and more supermarkets are offering organic produce.

of people who end up eating that meat. The growing of a single crop on a large farm can deplete the soil of its nutrients. In short, many people say, modern agribusiness does more harm than good.

AN OLD APPROACH

Some people say we need a new approach to agriculture and food production. They say we need to grow food and raise animals without harmful, human-made chemicals. That approach is called organic farming, but it's really an old approach, not a new one. In ancient times, all farmers were organic farmers. They used manure to fertilize crops. They used chrysanthemums and praying mantises to control pests naturally. They rotated crops to restore nutrients to the soil.

Launched in the late twentieth century, the modern organic farming movement has revived these ancient techniques. Around the world, thousands of organic farmers are raising food much the way their ancestors did. According to the Organic Trade Association, Americans spent almost $25 billion on organic foods in 2009. More than 11 percent of all the fruits and vegetables sold in the United States that year were organically grown. In 2008 nearly 5 million acres

At this organic farm near Bangor, Wisconsin, chickens roam freely outdoors. They eat healthy feed, with no chemical additives.

(2 million hectares) of U.S. farmland were dedicated to organic food. Around the world, nearly 1.4 million farmers in 154 countries use organic growing methods. Worldwide 86 million acres (35 million hectares) of land are farmed organically.

A TRIP BACK IN TIME

Most organic farms combine the best of modern and ancient technology. For instance, organic farmers use many ancient growing techniques, but they also employ gasoline-powered tractors and electric irrigation pumps. To really get a feel for ancient farming—with none of the modern enhancements—you'd need to visit a place like Butser Ancient Farm.

Butser Ancient Farm is in Hampshire County in southern England. At this "living history" farm, opened in 1974, visitors can experience English farm life as it was from about 400 B.C. to A.D. 400. The farm features haystacks, fences, kitchens, and storage sheds built with natural materials and ancient

▼ The round buildings at Butser Ancient Farm have thatched roofs—the same style used by English farmers two thousand years ago. At this living history farm, visitors can learn more about ancient farming.

methods. Farm animals include cattle, sheep, goats, and pigs, who spend their days grazing in open meadows. Farm staff members cultivate wheat, oats, barley, and rye in Butser's fields. Staffers have constructed farm buildings out of timber and thatch (matted straw and other plant materials), just as they would have been built in ancient times. Staffers even make iron farm tools in Butser's forge, or iron-making shop. They give tours to school groups and other visitors and sometimes enlist volunteers to help them with farm chores. They also give workshops on ancient carpentry techniques, medicinal herbs, pottery making, sheep shearing, and other ancient crafts.

Another living history farm is the Ioway Living History Farms in Urbandale, Iowa. This farm teaches visitors about the Ioway Indians, who lived in the region for thousands of years before the arrival of Europeans. These farmers raised corn, beans, and squash. They supplemented this food by hunting and fishing. At the Ioway farm, visitors can see three different kinds of Ioway houses—a cool summerhouse made of bark, a warmer house for winter made of cattail leaves, and a buffalo hide tepee, used for traveling. Visitors will also learn how the Ioway dried meat and other foods, prepared animal hides and furs, made stone tools, fired pottery, and grew gardens.

MODERN-DAY CAVE PEOPLE

For some people, revisiting ancient farming isn't enough. Some experts say we should take a lesson from our oldest ancestors, the earliest hunter-gatherers. In 2010 a biochemist and nutritionist named Robb Wolf published a book called *The Paleo Solution: The Original Human Diet.* The title comes from the name Paleolithic period, which lasted from about 2.5 million to about 10,000 years ago. Wolf says that people of the Paleolithic period ate the perfect diet, with just the right balance of meat, vegetables, and fat.

The typical Paleolithic diet was about 65 percent vegetables and 35 percent meat. The meat came from wild animals, which have less fat than animals raised on farms. The Paleolithic diet was high in plant fiber, which is good for digestion. It was also high in calcium (good for the bones) and vitamin C (good for overall health). Paleolithic people ate almost no sugar and very little salt. Wolf and others say that modern Americans could cut their risk for cancer, diabetes, heart disease, and obesity by adopting the diet of their hunter-gatherer ancestors.

Some people have put Wolf's ideas into practice. They eat only meat, vegetables, fruits, nuts, and other foods that would have been available to people during the Paleolithic period. They don't eat bread, since bread is a product of the agricultural revolution. They don't eat any food made from domesticated plants. Calling themselves cave people, some of Wolf's followers even exercise like hunter-gatherers. They leap from boulder to boulder and run short sprints—just like hunter-gatherers might have done while fleeing a charging animal. "Hunter-gatherers were tall, strong, and healthy," writes modern-day caveman John Durant. "Modern humans would be healthier if we ate the types of foods that existed in the wild before the advent of agriculture."

NO TURNING BACK

Of course, modern people can never really go back in time to the days of ancient farming—let alone the days of hunting and gathering—and most of us wouldn't want to. Making your own tools from stone, wood, or iron; grinding grain by hand; and skinning animals is hard and dirty work. Most modern readers are probably happy to pick up the food needed for dinner at the supermarket.

"Agriculture for an honorable and high-minded man, is the best of all occupations or arts by which men procure the means of living."

—Xenophon, ancient Greek historian, fourth century B.C.

But the ancient farming life had its benefits. People produced clean and nutritious foods with their own hands. They were resourceful. They knew how to fish and care for animals. They knew which plants were healthful and which were poisonous. In short, they knew how to live off the land.

Marcus Tullius Cicero, an ancient Roman orator and statesman, wrote, "For of all gainful professions, nothing is better, nothing more pleasing, nothing more delightful, nothing better becomes a well-bred man than agriculture." Certainly many ancient farmers—and probably many modern ones—would agree.

TIMELINE

CA. 400,000 B.C.	People in Europe first use fire to cook food.
CA. 14,000 B.C.	People in Japan make the first pottery vessels.
CA. 11,000 B.C.	The last ice age ends. As temperatures rise, stands of wild wheat grow in the Fertile Crescent in the Middle East.
CA. 10,000 B.C.	People in the ancient Middle East domesticate dogs and begin farming.
CA. 7000 B.C.	People in ancient China domesticate millet.
CA. 5000 B.C.	People in ancient Scandinavia invent barbed fishhooks. People in ancient Bolivia domesticate potatoes.
CA. 3500 B.C.	People in ancient Mesopotamia invent the potter's wheel.
CA. 3000 B.C.	People in ancient China begin eating with chopsticks. Ancient Egyptian rulers establish wine-making operations.
CA. 2500 B.C.	Ancient Egyptians build a dam across the Nile River to create an artificial lake. Ancient Egyptians began raising bees.
CA. 2300 B.C.	Ancient Egyptians build a canal to Lake Moeris to store excess water from the Nile River.
CA. 1700 B.C.	A Babylonian writer carves a series of recipes on two clay tablets.
CA. 800 B.C.	Ancient Chinese farmers begin planting rice in paddies.
CA. 700 B.C.	Ancient Greek farmers domesticate olive trees. Greek poet Homer writes *The Odyssey*, which describes Laertes' farm.
200S B.C.	The ancient Greek mathematician Archimedes invents the Archimedes' screw, a kind of water pump.
CA. 100 B.C.	Professional millers begin to grind grain with big millstones.

FIRST CENTURY A.D.	Farmers in Gaul invent the vallus for cutting stalks of grain.
CA. A.D. 100	Chinese farmers start using dried chrysanthemums to kill insects on vegetable plants.
CA. 300	People in ancient Japan and ancient India learn to make silk.
CA. 550	Emperor Justinian I of the Eastern Roman Empire sends spies to China to learn the secrets of silk making.
1793	U.S. inventor Eli Whitney invents the cotton gin.
1830s	U.S. inventor Cyrus McCormick invents a mechanical reaper.
1837	U.S. inventor John Deere invents the steel plow.
1860s	U.S. inventor Thomas Adams makes chewing gum out of chicle.
1974	The Butser Ancient Farm opens in Hampshire County, England.
1980S	Professor Daniel Fisher shows that ancient hunter-gatherers might have used underwater caching to keep meat from spoiling.
1994	Researchers at the University of Pennsylvania Museum find the oldest known wine jars. Dating from 5400 to 5000 B.C., the jars come from northern Iran.
2004	Other researchers at the University of Pennsylvania Museum of Archaeology and Anthropology find ancient liquor jars dating from 7000 to 6600 B.C. The jars had contained a fruity cocktail.
2010	Nutritionist Robb Wolf publishes *The Paleo Solution*, which argues that prehistoric people ate the most healthful diet.

GLOSSARY

AGRICULTURE: the science or occupation of growing crops and raising animals to get food and other products

AQUACULTURE: raising fish, shellfish, or edible sea plants in an artificial environment

ARCHAEOLOGIST: a scientist who studies the remains of past human cultures

ARTIFACT: a human-made object, especially one characteristic of a certain group or a historical period

BACTERIA: tiny organisms that might be helpful or harmful to humans. Some bacteria cause food to spoil. Others play a role in fermentation.

BIOLOGICAL PEST CONTROL: using living things and natural substances to kill insects and other pests that harm crops

BREED: to mate plants or animals with certain traits to produce offspring with those traits

CULTIVATE: to prepare farmland and grow crops

DOMESTICATE: to change wild animals and plants into varieties better suited for human use

DROUGHT: a long period of little or no rainfall

EXCAVATE: to dig into the earth, especially to search for ancient remains or artifacts

FERMENTATION: a chemical change in a substance caused by living organisms such as yeast or bacteria. People use fermentation to make wine, beer, cheese, bread, and other foods.

FERTILIZER: a substance added to the soil to help plants grow

HARVEST: to gather crops at the end of the growing season

HUNTER-GATHERERS: people who get food by hunting, fishing, and gathering wild plants

IRRIGATION: systems and tools for supplying crops with water

KILN: a large oven or furnace used for hardening pottery or bricks

NUTRIENTS: substances in food or soil, such as vitamins or minerals, that provide nourishment to animals or plants

ORGANIC FARMING: farming without using human-made chemicals to kill weeds, kill insects, or fertilize the soil

PUDDLING: flooding fields; a process used in China to grow rice

SCAVENGER: an animal that feeds on the remains of animals that have already been killed or died naturally

SLASH-AND-BURN AGRICULTURE: chopping down and burning trees on a plot of ground, then planting crops in the cleared land

SOURCE NOTES

12   Brian M. Fagan, ed., *The Seventy Great Inventions of the Ancient World* (London: Thames and Hudson, 2004), 113.

25   Jeremiah 31:5 (New International Version).

26–27   Yale University Library, Near East Collection, "Middle Eastern and Islamic Cuisine," Yale University Library Near East Collection, 2010, http://www.library.yale.edu/neareast/exhibitions/cuisine.html (September 24, 2010).

34   Herodotus, "The History of Herodotus," Internet Classics Archive, 1994–2009, http://classics.mit.edu/Herodotus/history.2.ii.html (September 24, 2010).

38   Felipe Fernández-Armesto, *Near a Thousand Tables: A History of Food* (New York: Free Press, 2002), 91.

41–42   Peter James and Nick Thorpe, *Ancient Inventions* (New York: Ballantine Books, 1994), 396.

55   Bernal Díaz Del Castillo, *The Memoirs of the Conquistador Bernal Diaz Del Castillo*, vol 1. (London: J. Hatchard and Son, 1844), 230.

60   Homer, *The Odyssey of Homer*, trans. Richmond Lattimore (New York: HarperCollins, 1999), 351.

61   Ibid., 114.

66   Patent Pending Blog, "The Roman Era Grain Harvester," Patent Pending Blog, October 3, 2005, http://patentpending.blogs.com/patent_pending_blog/2005/10/the_roman_era_g.html (September 24, 2010).

68   Patrick Faas, "Eight Recipes from around the Roman Table," University of Chicago Press, 2003, http://www.press.uchicago.edu/Misc/Chicago/233472.html (September 24, 2010).

68   Tryon Edwards, *A Dictionary of Thoughts* (Detroit: F. B. Dickerson, 1908), 348.

82   John Durant, "Why Hunter-Gatherers?" Hunter-Gatherer, n.d., http://hunter-gatherer.com/why-hunter-gatherers (September 24, 2010).

82   Thinkexist.com, "Agriculture Quotes," Thinkexist.com, http://pen.thinkexist.com/quotes/with/keyword/agriculture/ (September 24, 2010).

83   Ibid.

SELECTED BIBLIOGRAPHY

Diamond, Jared. *Guns, Germs, and Steel: The Fates of Human Societies.* New York: W. W. Norton and Company, 1999.

Fagan, Brian M., ed. *Discovery! Unearthing the New Treasures of Archaeology.* London: Thames and Hudson, 2007.

——. *The Seventy Great Inventions of the Ancient World.* London: Thames and Hudson, 2004.

Ferdández-Armesto, Felipe. *Near a Thousand Tables: A History of Food.* New York: Free Press, 2002.

Friedman, Paul, ed. *Food: The History of Taste.* Berkeley: University of California Press, 2007.

Hanson, Victor Davis. *The Other Greeks: The Family Farm and the Agrarian Roots of Western Civilization.* New York: Free Press, 1995.

James, Peter, and Nick Thorpe. *Ancient Inventions.* New York: Ballantine Books, 1994.

Kurlansky, Mark. *Choice Cuts: A Savory Selection of Food Writing from around the World and throughout History.* New York: Ballantine Books, 2002.

Salzberg, Hugh W. *From Caveman to Chemist.* Washington, DC: American Chemical Society Press, 1991.

Smith, Bruce D. *The Emergence of Agriculture.* New York: Scientific American Library, 1995.

Toussaint-Samat, Maguelonne. *A History of Food.* Cambridge, MA: Blackwell Reference, 1993.

Turner, Jack. *Spice: The History of Temptation.* New York: Alfred A. Knopf, 2004.

Visser, Margaret. *Much Depends on Dinner.* New York: Grove Press, 1986.

FURTHER READING

Friedman, Lauri S. *Organic Food and Farming*. Farmington Hills, MI:
Greenhaven Press, 2009.
Ancient farmers were the first organic farmers. In modern times, some
people believe that organic farming can alleviate many problems,
including world hunger and environmental degradation. Others disagree.
This book contains essays from various authors, who examine all sides
of the organic farming debate.

Gifford, Clive. *Food and Cooking in Ancient Greece*. New York: PowerKids
Press, 2010.
The ancient Greeks ate well, on a diet rich in olives, figs, and cheeses. In
this book, you'll learn about the culture of ancient Greece as well as the
cuisine. You'll even find recipes for some ancient Greek dishes.

Jango-Cohen, Judith. *The History of Food*. Minneapolis: Lerner Publications
Company, 2006.
How did people get food in earlier eras? They had to hunt it, gather
it, grow it, and process it themselves. But over the centuries, new
technology made it easier and easier for people to get food. This book
looks at food through the ages.

Keoke, Emory Dean. *Food, Farming, and Hunting*. New York: Facts on File,
2005.
Some of the world's favorite foods—including chocolate, potatoes,
tomatoes, and avocados—originated in the Americas. Find out how
ancient Americans hunted, gathered, and raised the food they needed.

Passport to History series. Minneapolis: Twenty-First Century Books,
2001–2004.
In this series, readers will take trips back in time to ancient China,
Egypt, Greece, Rome, and the Mayan civilization. They will learn about
people's clothing, foods, work, and other aspects of daily life.

Steele, Philip, and John Farndon. *Mesopotamia.* New York: DK Children, 2007.

> The ancient Mesopotamians were leaders in agricultural technology. They were the first farmers and herders. They invented tools and techniques for raising and processing food. With colorful illustrations, this book sheds light on ancient Mesopotamian culture.

Unearthing Ancient Worlds series. Minneapolis: Twenty-First Century Books, 2008–2009.

> This series takes readers on journeys of discovery, as archaeologists discover King Tut's tomb, the royal Incan city of Machu Picchu, the ruins of Pompeii, and other archaeological treasures.

Visual Geography Series. Minneapolis: Twenty-First Century Books, 2003–2011.

> Each book in this series examines one country, with lots of information about its ancient history. The series' companion website—vgsbooks .com—offers free, downloadable material and links to sites with additional information about each country.

Whitman, Sylvia. *What's Cooking? The History of American Food.* Minneapolis: Twenty-First Century Books, 2001.

> Discover the foods that Americans of every era have planted, harvested, and prepared. This book provides information on everything from the corn that Native Americans grew and ate to modern-day fast food burgers and frozen meals.

Woods, Michael, and Mary B Woods. Seven Wonders of the Ancient World set. Minneapolis: Twenty-First Century Books, 2009.

> This set of seven titles explores Herodotus's list of the seven ancient wonders as well as magnificent buildings and monuments from ancient Africa, Asia, Central and South America, and North America.

WEBSITES

HISTORY OF POTATOES

http://whatscookingamerica.net/History/PotatoHistory.htm
This site traces the history of the potato, from its origins in ancient
South America to modern dinner tables. You'll also find links to recipes
and even famous quotes about potatoes.

HISTORY OF SILK

http://www.silk-road.com/artl/silkhistory.shtml
This Web page from the Silkroad Foundation introduces the history of
silk making in China and the profitable ancient silk trade.

PEARLS

http://www.fieldmuseum.org/pearls/exhibition.html
Pearls were prized in ancient times, just as they are in modern times.
This website from the Field Museum in Chicago explains how oysters
make pearls and how people interfere with nature to make even more
pearls.

SHEEP 101.INFO

http://www.sheep101.info/
shearing.html
Ancient people relied on
sheep for milk, meat, and
wool. This website tells
you everything you always
wanted to know about
sheep—and more.

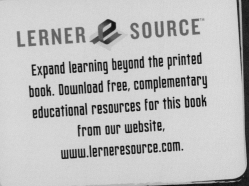

LERNER e SOURCE™

Expand learning beyond the printed
book. Download free, complementary
educational resources for this book
from our website,
www.lernersource.com.

INDEX

agribusiness, 77–79
agricultural revolution, 19, 20–21, 27
Americas, 6, 48–57; agriculture's effect on society, 49; beans, 50–51, 53, 57; chewing gum, 53–54; chocolate, 54; corn, 52, 53, 57; guinea pigs, 56–57; llamas and alpacas, 55–56; slash-and-burn agriculture, 51–52
animals, domesticated, 17–18, 22, 33, 55–57: goats and sheet, 22, 33; guinea pigs, 56–57; large draft animals, 23; llamas and alpacas, 55–56
aquaculture, 43–44, 66–67
Andeans, 55–57
Archimedes' screw, 61–62
Assyrians, 21
Aztecs, 48, 49

Babylonians, 21, 26–27
beans, 50–51, 53, 57, 65
beekeeping, 34–35
biological pest control, 40–42
bread, 26, 62, 82. *See also* grain
breeding, 22, 31, 55–56, 72, 77

Central America, 51–54
chewing gum, 53–54
China, 6, 38–47: aquaculture, 43–44; biological pest control, 40–42; first ice cream, 47; mixed-stock rearing, 42–43; puddling rice, 39–40; tea, 47
chocolate, 54, 74
cookbooks, 26–27, 68
corn. *See* grain
crop rotation, 52–53, 72, 79

Dark Ages. *See* Middle Ages

diet. *See* nutrition
dogs, 17–18
domestication: of animals, 17–18, 22, 33, 55–57; of bees, 34–35; of llamas and alpacas, 55–56; of plants, 18, 49, 50; of rice, 38–40; of silkworm moth, 44–45; of wheat, 38
dye, clothing, 30–31

Egypt, 32–37; beekeeping, 34–35; beer and wine making, 35–36; irrigation system, 33–34; spices, 37
equipment, farm, 75–77

fabrics, 29–30
fermentation, 28, 35–36
fertilization, 42–43, 78
fish farming, 66–67
fishing, 10, 13–14, 59
food preparation, 25–28; fermentation, 28; first cookbook, 26–27; kitchens, 25–26; ovens, 26
food preservation, 15–16, 70, 71

gardens, 24
goats and sheep, 22, 33
grain, 20–21; corn, 48, 52, 53, 57; flax, 33; making bread, 26; millet, 33; milling, 62–63; reaping, 65–66; rice, 38–40, 43; wheat, 33, 60, 65
Greece, 58–63; Archimedes' screw, 61–62; bread making, 62; irrigation systems, 61–62; milling grain, 62–63; wine, 60, 61
guinea pigs, 56–57

honey, 15, 34–35, 62

hunter-gatherers, 6, 10–19, 48, 81–82:
fishing, 10, 13–14; food preservation,
15–16; food storage, 14–16

ice, 69, 71
ice cream, 47
Incas. *See* Andeans
insect control, 40–42
irrigation methods: in the Americas,
52, 57; in China, 40; in Egypt, 33–34;
in Greece, 61–62; in the Middle East,
24–25

"living history" farms, 80–81
llamas and alpacas, 55–56

Maya, 49, 51–54
Mesopotamia, 21, 23, 24–25, 26–30
Mexico, 49, 50–54
Middle Ages, 72
Middle East, 20–31; domestication of
goats and sheep, 22; fabrics, 29–30;
fermentation, 28; irrigation methods,
24–25; kitchens, 25–26; looms, 30;
plows, 23; pottery, 27–28; Tyrian
purple dye, 30–31; wine, 28
mixed-stock rearing, 42–43

nutrition: corn and beans,
complementary nature of, 53;
Paleolithic diet, 81–82; Roman diet, 67

olive oil, 60
organic farming, 79–80

ovens, 26
oxen, 23, 33, 76

Paleolithic diet, 81–82
pearls, 43–44
Phoenicians, 30
plow, 23, 33, 65, 72, 76
pottery, 27–28

Renaissance, 73–74
rice. *See* grain
Rome, 64–71; farming, 65; fish farming,
66–67; ice, 69, 71; reaping grain,
65–66; salt, 70; spices, 69

salt, 70, 82
sapodilla trees, 53
silk, 44–46
slash-and-burn agriculture, 51–52
South America, 49, 55–57
spices, 37, 69
Sumerians, 21

tea, 47
technology: agricultural, 6–9; ancient
roots, 5–9; defined, 4–5
tobacco, 74

utensils, eating, 11, 42, 59

wheat. *See* grain
wine, 28, 35–36, 60, 61

ABOUT THE AUTHORS

Michael Woods is a science and medical journalist in Washington, D.C. He has won many national writing awards. Mary B. Woods is a school librarian. Their past books include the fifteen-volume Disasters Up Close series, the seven-volume Seven Wonders of the Ancient World set, and the seven-volume Seven Wonders of the Natural World set. The Woodses have four children. When not writing, reading, or enjoying their grandchildren, the Woodses travel to gather material for future books.

PHOTO ACKNOWLEDGMENTS

The images in this book are used with the permission of: © Erich Lessing/Art Resource, NY, pp. 3, 20-21, 21, 29; © Laura Westlund/Independent Picture Service, pp. 4-5; © G. Dagli Orti/De Agostini Picture Library/Learning Pictures, p. 7; The Art Archive/Gianni Dagli Orti, p. 8; © INTERFOTO/Alamy, p. 9; © Suzanne Long/Alamy, p. 10; © Pascal Goetgheluck/Photo Researchers, Inc., p. 12; © Sissie Brimberg/National Geographic/Getty Images, p. 13; © Prehistoric/The Bridgeman Art Library/Getty Images, pp. 14, 27; © Egyptian/The Bridgeman Art Library/Getty Images, p. 17; © De Agostini Picture Library/Learning Pictures, p. 18; © Werner Forman/Art Resource, NY, pp. 22, 46; © North Wind Picture Archives, p. 24; The Granger Collection, New York, pp. 25, 38-39, 48, 77 (top); The Art Archive/British Museum/Alfredo Dagli Orti, p. 26; © Carpe Diem-Egypt/Alamy, pp. 32-33; The Art Archive/Bibliothèque Musée du Louvre/Gianni Dagli Orti, p. 33; © Dr. Kenneth J. Stein, p. 35; © S. Vannini/De Agostini Picture Library/Learning Pictures, p. 36; Pete Oxford/DanitaDelimont.com/Newscom, p. 40; © iStockphoto.com/esolla, p. 41; © iStockphoto.com/Floortje, p. 42; © Feng Hui/Dreamstime.com, p. 43; © Seesea/Dreamstime.com, p. 44; Hermitage, St. Petersburg, Russia/Photo © Boltin Picture Library/The Bridgeman Art Library, p. 45; © José Antonio Sánchez Poy/Dreamstime.com, p. 50; © Paul Edmondson/Stone/Getty Images, p. 51; © British Museum/Werner Forman Archive/The Image Works, p. 52; © Bohemian Nomad Picturemakers/CORBIS, p. 54; © William J Herbert/Stone/Getty Images, p. 55; © iStockphoto.com/Danny Warren, p. 56; © SEF/Art Resource, NY, pp. 58-59; © The Trustees of The British Museum/Art Resource, NY, p. 60; © C.M. Dixon/Ancient Art & Architecture Collection, Ltd., p. 63; Santa Costanza, Rome, Italy/The Bridgeman Art Library, pp. 64-65; © Alan Collins/Alamy, p. 65; © R. Sheridan/Ancient Art & Architecture Collection, Ltd., p. 66; © MARKA/Alamy, p. 67; © Scala/Art Resource, NY, pp. 68, 69; © Bildarchiv Preussischer Kulturbesitz/Art Resource, NY, pp. 72-73; © National Trust Photo Library/Art Resource, NY, p. 75; © The Print Collector/Alamy, p. 76; © Josiah Davidson/Photographer's Choice/Getty Images, p. 77 (bottom); © iStockphoto.com/syagci, p. 78; © Macduff Everton/CORBIS, p. 79; © Derek Croucher/AA World Travel/Topfoto/The Image Works, p. 80.

Front cover: © AFP/Getty Images (top left); © The Bridgeman Art Library/Getty Images (top right); © Alexey Stiop/Alamy (bottom).